"Being a mom is tough, but it's wonderful, funny, and the most exhausting thing ever. Dineen captures this humor-bordering-on-despair with an acute sense of comedic timing and a keen awareness of the often nonsensical world that is raising kids in modern society."

—San Francisco Book Review, 5-stars

". . . Whitney's book, her voice, and experiences shared [are] hilarious but also raw, honest, and beautiful. I highly recommend *Motherhood Martyrdom & Costco Runs*. It is a fun, easy read, but is also realistic. If taken to heart and mind, this book can help drive you to do good in the world and in your own personal life as a mother and as a person."

—Portland Book Review

"Whitney Dineen serves up an honest and hilarious portrayal of motherhood. Motherhood is tough and you're going to laugh or cry; you should always choose to laugh."

—Jen Mann, NYT Bestselling Author of My Lame Life

"Erma [Bombeck] would probably get the biggest charge out of *Motherhood Martyrdom & Costco Runs*. It's beautifully written and a joy to read, even the parts that are embarrassing for some Victorian throwbacks like the author's husband. Dineen works a bit of magic here in this authentic, inspiring and very human collection of humorist writing. *Motherhood Martyrdom & Costco Runs* is most highly recommended."

—Jack Mangus for Readers' Favorite, 5-stars

"Laugh-out-loud funny, endearing, and so spot-on!"

—**Bestselling Author, Becky Monson**

"With *Motherhood Martyrdom and Costco Runs*, Whitney Dineen has given us a beautiful, comical, and often poignant look into what raising children is really like. I found myself laughing and shedding a tear or two as I devoured the pages of this fantastic book. I absolutely adored it. And now I'm off to renew my membership at Costco!"

—**Bestselling Author, Jennifer Peel**

"Dineen and I are kindred spirits - modern day mothers who tell it like it is. She beautifully expresses her successes and failures as a mother, while making us all feel a little better about our own parenting failures. Although we are very similar - I applaud her ability to have a 5 & 7 year old that have only ever heard her say the word "hell." This is what I call a GREAT mother!! This is a great read for anyone with children - and is looking for a light-hearted, humorous take on the reality that is parenting today."

—**Blogger, Laydee Googoogaga**

"A must read for every seasoned, new and expecting mother. Whitney shares her journey through motherhood with such raw honesty that will make you laugh, cry and possibly even tinkle a little."

—**Book Mama Blog**

"I have one word of advice for anyone preparing to read *Motherhood Martyrdom and Costco Runs* before they get started: use care where you read this book. The reason is simple. You see, you are likely to laugh out loud . . . repeatedly. As laughter makes for good medicine, I encourage you to grab your copy of this little gem soon. We could all use a little humor and a little healing!"

—**Patricia Reding for Readers' Favorite, 5-stars**

"...seriously this book is hilarious! I mean if I was [reading it] in public and people saw me they would think that I have lost my mind!"

—Bethany Clark, Books and Wine are Lovely

"Whitney explains motherhood in a way that all moms, young, old and in-between, can relate too. This book is a fabulous inside look at all the things we hope no other more seemingly put together mother will notice."

—Aimee Brown, For the Love of Chick Lit

"Whitney Dineen keeps the parenting struggle real. Each chapter is like a Costco sample, you'll keep coming back for more super-size laughs and a jumbo dose of honesty."

—Barbara Kahn, Baer Books

Motherhood Martyrdom
and
Costco Runs

Whitney Dineen

Published in the United States by Thirty-Three Partners Publishing.

Library of Congress Cataloguing-In-Publication Data
Dineen, Whitney
Motherhood Martyrdom & Costco Runs: a memoir / Whitney Dineen
ISBN: 978-0-9988620-0-2

Other Books by Whitney Dineen

Romantic Comedies

She Sins at Midnight
The Reinvention of Mimi Finnegan
Mimi Plus Two

Middle Reader Adventures

Wilhelmina and the Willamette Wig Factory
Who the Heck is Harvey Stingle?
Beware of the Basement (Coming in the fall of 2017)

Children's Books

The Friendship Bench

This book is dedicated to
all you breeders out there.

Contents

Author's Acknowledgments

A million thanks to my family and friends for being a part of my rollercoaster ride into motherhood. I'm not sure I would have ever made it without you!

To my husband, Jimmy, you're an amazing husband and wonderful daddy to our littles, and I'm thrilled to be on this journey with you! You're also a lot of fun to tease. Sorry I had to rat out some of your peculiarities (I cite ding ding and your extra finger), but they were irresistible.

Mom and Dad, I adore you! I'd probably still call child protective services on you, but please know that it's nothing personal. I'm full of gratitude for everything you've done for me and continue to do for me. Who knew I'd be such a handful?

Dearest family and friends that I've used for fodder, you're welcome for changing your names. I know you're probably going to try to distance yourselves from me now, but I'm going to cling to you like wet toilet paper on the bottom of your shoe, so don't bother.

To my readers, I love you! Thank you for getting me and reading me and supporting me. I know you're probably just doing it because you're relieved there's someone out there crazier than you are, but that's cool. I'm not going to look a gift horse in the mouth.

To my writing buddies, Becky Monson, Jennifer Peel, Kathryn Biel, and Rich Amooi: who knew I could be so needy? A million thanks for your patience, advice, and friendship; they mean the world!

I'm lucky enough to be a part of several online writing groups which offer endless author resources. I'm thankful to all of them, but to Tracie Banister and my other friends at Chick Lit Chat, you continue to be the best support around!

Marlene Engel and Paula Bothwell, thank you for making me sound semi-literate by offering your proofreading skills. I'd be lost without you.

Karan Eleni, you rock socks like a fox eating lox on a box! Thank you for all your hard work on my website and every other thing you do for me.

Thank you to my dear friend, Jen Ward. I can honestly say I tried very hard not to write this book, but you're such a big nag, I had to. Now that it's done, I'm really glad you were so pushy. There's nothing like honest reflection to make you grateful for all the stops on your journey. And above all else, I am grateful!

Introduction

This book is titled Motherhood Martyrdom and Costco Runs for one obvious reason. If you happen to be a mother of young children, you know your life is either spent hanging on the cross of said motherhood or running your entire brood to Costco for more toilet paper. It's who we are.

Many of the moms from my childhood were the stay at home variety. These ladies gave up a lot of personal and professional desires to be Johnny-on-the-spot for the home front. They scheduled everything from doctor's appointments to music lessons to extracurricular activities. They made sure the wash was done, the house was clean, and meals were put on the table.

My mom found ways to express herself and cultivate her interests within the confines of her role as the CEO of our family. She wrote an article for a local Chicago paper and taught gourmet cooking classes. She did yoga with her friends and ran the hospital auxiliary. She also entertained on a grand scale and kept a big garden. She was one busy lady.

Today, most households require two incomes to function properly. We're scrambling in a million different directions trying to get everyone everywhere they need to be, and still the laundry needs to get done, the house needs to be cleaned, groceries have to be purchased and then there's basic yard maintenance, so your neighbors don't rat you out to the homeowners' association for neglected weeds and an unruly lawn. And darn if your kids don't expect you to feed them every day! Add making a living and the full social and academic calendars of children and what do you have? The answer is very tired parents.

I'm not saying parenthood was easier for my folks. Having children, no matter the generation, is full of highs and lows, stresses, and worries. Kids are a gigantic, wonderful, exhausting, excruciating endeavor. And they are worth every harrowing second of the journey.

This is a book about my rollercoaster ride into middle-aged motherhood. There are self-pitying tales of dirty clothes and dishes, sleepless nights and bad hair. I regularly nail myself to the martyrdom cross and occasionally come down and get real. I laugh at my kids and I love them. I share the good, the bad, and the ugly. I also go to Costco, a lot.

These vignettes are all relatively quick reads as I know you're most likely enjoying them on the toilet or in the three-and-a-half minutes you can still focus at the end of the day. I figure if you block out five minutes a day, you can have this book finished in a month. Hopefully, at the end you'll have had some laughs, perhaps a couple of tears, and an eye roll or two. I'm guessing you'll also feel a lot better about yourself as a mother, because the truth is, no one makes motherhood look harder than I do.

It's All Relative

I used to think I'd have all the children I was going to have by the time I was thirty. Then thirty hit and I didn't have any so I adjusted my deadline to forty. By the time I was thirty-seven I was having miscarriages every ten to twelve months. That's when my deadline turned into more of a plea. It went something like, "Dear God, please let me hatch out one or two of these eggs, successfully, before they're all hardboiled. Please!"

Then the negotiating started. "God, if you let me have kids, I'll be less vain. I'll donate eighty percent of everything I own to charity. I'll give up french fries for life!" We all know I couldn't possibly hold up my end of this deal, especially the french fry thing, but I was desperate enough to mean it at the time.

I never wanted to be an old mother. I wanted to be a young, cool, hip mom that all the kids wanted to hang with. They'd clamor to me like barnacles on a boat just to learn the secret of my awesomeness. They'd bask in my magnificence like Oregonians on the first sunny day after a long winter's rain.

Ultimately, two things made my dream unattainable. One, I've never been cool. I've acted and dressed like a forty-year-old since I was fifteen. Young, I could be, but hip was never in the cards. Number two, I had my first live birth at forty. You know, the age some are experiencing a rapidly emptying nest, freedom to travel the world, and large enough bank accounts/investment portfolios/IRAs to buy Porsches and other sundry toys they've always longed for.

Aside from not being perceived as the cool parent, my other concern about old motherhood was how I'd cope as the geriatric crone in a pack of young hens. Would I be able to find friends? Would the cool moms shut me out like a freak pledging the wrong sorority? Would they keep forgetting I was my child's mother and not her grandmother?

It turns out, my fears were for naught. Apparently, age has very little to do with how we deal with motherhood. My mom friends range in age from thirty-two to fifty-two and here's the fundamental truth about all of us: we're all overwhelmed, we're all tired, we all scream at our kids, and we all dream of a clean house.

Here's the difference. Some of the young moms actually leave their domiciles looking like they've brushed their hair and teeth. Some even wear clean clothes. Some have the energy and desire to fit into their pre-baby jeans and go to yoga regularly in their delightfully patterned LuLaRoe leggings.

Conversely, the forty-eight-year-old mother of two young grade schoolers will often wake up, look down at the faded Old Navy yoga pants she slept in, and deem them clean enough for another day. She'll use coffee to mask her morning breath and somehow putting on makeup will devolve into making sure the most noticeable chin hairs get plucked. Yes, she will occasionally fall into downward dog, but that mostly has to do with tipping over, and not actual yoga.

Two of my older daughter's BFFs have moms that are the same age as me and I find this enormously comforting. We're drawn to each other at school functions and are gladdened by the knowledge there's another in the room old enough to know who Edith Bunker is. Sometimes we'll throw out band names like Devo or Depeche Mode for the same reason. After all, actually being sixteen when *Sixteen Candles* came out is way different than watching it only after it had earned retro cult classic status.

I guess what I'm really trying to say is this: the age you are when you become a mother is irrelevant. There will always be younger, cooler, hipper, thinner women than you. But you can bet your butt if these women also happen to be mothers, they're just as tired and frustrated as you are. It's all relative.

Meanwhile, Somewhere
Back in the Colonies

Imagine accidentally slipping through a crack in the space/time continuum and falling smack into Colonial America, sometime circa the American Revolution. Now envision yourself walking down a picturesque tree-lined brick street and strolling into a quaint little mercantile. The offerings are unimaginably modest by our modern day standards, but no one seems to notice. Our forefathers/mothers are bustling around purchasing necessities like tea, sugar, and muslin. You with me?

Okay, now imagine striking up a conversation with someone. You know, "Hey there, how's it going? Seen any Red Coats in the area lately?" that kind of thing. Once you've established a thread of comradery, I want you to try to explain Costco to this person. I'm just going to pause to give you a moment to try to conjure such an insane vision.

If it were me, I think I'd start with, "You should see what the stores look like where I come from. We have this one called Costco that's about ten thousand times the size of this store. I mean it's HUGE!" Then I'd launch into all the crazy stuff you can buy at Costco. "They don't sell fabric because the clothes are already made and they're available in every size you can imagine. They even sell shoes, socks, and unmentionables. And the books, SO many books!"

I'd steer clear of talking about the photo and computer departments, lest they hang me for witchcraft. But I'd make sure to venture into all the glassware, bakeware, and dish selections. Not to mention the assortment of fruits, vegetables, bakery items, and jewelry. Then I'd hit them with, "They sell hundreds of chickens already killed, plucked, roasted, and ready to eat!" I'd regale them with tales of their succulence. "They're the most tender and juicy birds you've ever put in your mouth. Did I mention they were already dead?"

I'd expound upon the wonders of the dairy department and the insane cheese assortment. I'm pretty sure the baking aisle would leave them swooning like debutantes at their coming out balls. Sugar and flour in twenty-five pound bags, chocolate chips, cocoa, and spices. The hardest part would be keeping the wall of toilet paper to myself. I mean, how in the world would a denizen of Colonial America ever begin to imagine the wonders of toilet paper, yet alone an entire wall of the stuff?

I'd elaborate on the nuts next. "They have every kind of nut you can imagine: pine nuts, peanuts, walnuts, almonds, pecans, pistachio, macadamia nuts, and cashews! And they're already shelled, roasted, and salted and some are even covered in chocolate!" I'd gush.

There's no way to describe Costco without mentioning the samples. "They sell food from all over the world and give you samples of it in almost every aisle you walk down, FREE!"

Then I'd wax poetic about all the wonderful medicines and

supplements available. I'd touch on the luxurious toiletries and hygiene products. When they were near to unconsciousness from the effort of trying to grasp such an Eden, I'd hit them with the food court. "They have slices of pizza as big as your head and the most decadent ice cream bars that have been dipped in melted chocolate and rolled in chopped nuts. There are machines that dispense every kind of drink you'd ever want! Don't get me started on the churros and soft serve frozen yogurt." Not that they'd know what any of these foods are. I don't recall ever hearing the colonials were known for their 'za or soft serve.

On and on I'd go until they'd either arrest me for heresy or lock me up for lunacy, although I usually pull myself out of this reverie before coming to any real harm. Mostly because I'm craving a frozen yogurt and have a burning hot desire to add another one hundred and sixty-eight rolls of toilet paper to my growing stash. Time for a Costco run!

I Walked Barefoot in the Snow!

"We didn't even have *stickers* when I was your age. Do you hear me? NO stickers!" I beseech my young daughters to grasp how incredibly fortunate they are to live in such a gluttonous loot-filled age. The fact that they have drawers full of stickers they don't properly revere is beyond me. I would have weeded the entire garden for the whole summer and given up my meager allowance for a year, just to have a tenth of what they take for granted as their due.

"What do you mean you didn't have stickers?" my seven-year-old demands. "You mean stickers weren't invented yet or you just didn't have any?"

"I mean," I say, trying to slow down my rapidly accelerating heart rate, "stickers were a thing only teachers had and they used them sparingly. Stickers were not available for children to buy. Do you hear me? NO STICKERS!"

My daughters stare at me like I'm saying the world was in black and white when I grew up. They have absolutely no barometer for a world devoid of stickers.

My five-year-old starts to speak very slowly as though any false movement might launch me into space like a bottle rocket. "Mommy," she enunciates carefully, "why didn't you just drive to the Dollar Store and buy stickers?"

"Why didn't I just drive to the Dollar Store?! Because," and I pause for dramatic effect here, "we didn't have Dollar Stores when I was a kid! Do you hear that, NO STICKERS and NO DOLLAR STORES?!"

It's like I'm telling them I'm from Mars or that I breathe through my toes, like I'm sharing I grew up in a land that didn't have sunshine or french fries. They simply do not know what to make of this confession. After what feels like eons of mentally dissecting me with their adorable big brown eyes and tilted heads, my seven-year-old comes over and throws her arms around me and consoles, "Oh, Mommy, that must have been so hard for you. I'm so sorry!"

Wait, what just happened here? I'm not bemoaning the lack of stickers in my formative years. I'm simply trying to get them to grasp how very lucky they are to have so much. So I try a new tactic. "We didn't have home computers when I was your age."

The five-year-old begs to know, "How did you print out coloring pages?"

How in the world do I begin to explain the seventies and eighties to these children? Their lives are so full of advantage and stuff they can't begin to conceive how great life was when things were a little harder to come by. I'm determined to make them appreciate the bounty in which they live.

So I try again. "You know how you have an iPad with all those great apps on it?" Then I innumerate some just in case they've forgotten, "There are Barbie makeover apps, baking apps, cake decorating apps, and the honey bee game?"

Two little heads nod up and down, so I continue. "We had

one electronic game. ONE. It plugged into our TV and the whole thing was two lines hitting a little electronic ball back and forth across the screen."

Seven asks, "What was the point of that?"

Five inquires, "Did it sing songs or flash bright colors? Did it bake anything?"

"No. It did nothing but knock a little ball back and forth across the screen. Well, actually it beeped every time it hit the ball, so it did that, too."

Again with the big brown eyes and tilting heads. "Why in the world would you want to play a game like that?" they demand to know.

"We played it for hours. We loved it! It was advanced technology in the seventies. Pong was the most amazing game EVER!" I can't believe I'm even saying that. I scoff at Pong, but I'm trying to put this into some perspective for my kids.

I know I'm moments away from telling them I walked to school barefoot in the snow, uphill both ways, with boulders on my shoulders. And that's when it hits me. I already have. A lack of stickers and Pong are my generation's barefoot in the snow. All of a sudden I feel a great kinship with my parents. I also feel very old.

Finding the Balance

I've long struggled to find balance in my life and the struggle is real, folks! According to my calculations, I need a minimum of thirty-six hours in a day and approximately nine point seven days in a week to accomplish everything necessary for optimal equilibrium. In order to be the mom, wife, daughter, writer, and friend I aspire to be, I'd need two clones, a cleaning lady, and a cook. In short, I'm screwed.

I have friends who assure me that taking care of myself first is the key to successful balance. "If you do too much for others and don't do for yourself, you'll wither on the vine!" (Or some equally inane nonsense.) I'm torn between wanting to hug them for their astonishing naiveté and smacking them senseless for wasting even a second of my life with such stupid drivel. "Me time" is something that was snatched from my grasp by wide-awake infants in the middle of the night, by norovirus spewed on freshly painted walls, and by constant butt wipings during the potty training years. I'm pretty sure "me time" is a mythical entity right up there with unicorns and fairies.

I was so sure when both of my girls hit full-day school, I'd have my life back; I would have the illusive "me time" we wax on about. My house would always be clean, I would write three times as many books, and everyone in my sphere would feel the full force of my presence. What a load of horse hooey!

Both girls have been in full-day school since September and I am no more productive for it. That's not entirely true. I actually go to the gym three mornings a week now and feel marginally healthier/less snatchy, so that's a good thing. The house is cleaner, but only because the mess makers aren't in constant whirl. And, I occasionally get to talk to an old friend on the phone. But sadly, I'm still buried under the weight of my "to-do" list. How am I ever going to find the balance I crave?

One friend suggested hot yoga as the cure-all. She's currently in traction, or would be if I had any telekinetic powers. I'm forty-eight. I'm as hot as I ever want to be again this side of a boiling pit of lava. Her suggestion is right up there with proposing the key to world peace is through regular mani-pedis or perhaps group hugs. Can you just see the start of every U.N. pow-wow starting with downward dog in a ninety-eight degree room, followed by OPI's "I'm Not Really a Waitress" painted on everyone's toes? Ludicrous.

I just returned home from a very informative writers' conference and couldn't wait to get back and start implementing all the marvelous new techniques I learned about. I learned that even if I have to force productivity, I *have* to be productive, that organization and involvement in social media can make or break me. I learned the faster I publish my books, the more momentum my career will have. Essentially, I learned that I will never be the huge success I dream of being if I don't give my career two hundred percent. Every. Single. Day.

I dwell on that when I'm making my littles their breakfast and packing their lunches. I worry about it when I pick them up from school and take them to the bounce house instead of coming home so I can go back to work. And when we're cuddled up in my bed at night watching the *Next Food Network Star*, I finally realize who cares? My girls don't care if I'm a household name or not. They don't care if all the laundry is perfectly folded in their drawers. They don't even care if my gray roots are dyed in a timely fashion. All they care about is that I'm present with them, actively participating in their lives.

In a ditch effort to save my sanity, I've decided to prioritize the various compartments of my world. My children come first. My husband is somewhere near the top of the list, but I often say to him, "Remember those twenty years we had together before having kids? Cling to the memories!" I don't even know what to say to my parents except, "Man, did I take you guys for granted!" And then comes work, laundry, vacuuming, shopping for groceries, etc.

I've come to the conclusion that balance is probably not something I will ever attain in a single period in my life. The hope is that at the end of my journey, I'll realize it was something that developed along the way. I envision sitting under a big oak tree with a good book, an afghan, and a mocha, sometime in the distant future, with a smile on my wrinkled face, reminiscing, "I've had a clean house, I've had wonderful times with friends, and I've written a lot of good stories along the way. But more importantly, I raised two kind and compassionate children who helped make the world a better place. I've had a successful and loving marriage and I was a good daughter. As a whole, I balanced a lot and did a pretty darn good job of it."

For now though, I'm a hectic mess just taking it one day at a time.

I Swear!

I love to swear. Some righteous judgmental twits will tell you swearing is a sign of a limited vocabulary or lack of intellect. They're wrong. Swearing is a marvelously freeing way to release the pressures of life. It's like working out without all the sweat and effort. It's genius!

Here's the thing though: as much as I love to let loose an array of vulgarities salty enough to leave the preacher's wife gasping for breath, I was forced to give it up. When I was pregnant with my older daughter, once it looked like the pregnancy was a go, my husband approached me and lovingly suggested I quit expressing myself like a sailor on shore leave.

I countered that I would give it up before our daughter started talking. He protested my timeline, stating there was no way I could go from my daily quota of filth to nothing, cold turkey. He was convinced I needed to cease immediately so it would be fully out of my system before our child arrived on the planet.

I wanted to tell him he was wrong. I could stop any time I wanted to. It's not like I was an addict. I can hear your eyes rolling. Yes, I know, the addict is ALWAYS the last to know.

But it's not like I was addicted to drugs, alcohol, or Ho Hos.

I was addicted to expression. How can that be wrong? I offered to institute a swear jar and promised to happily pay every time an expletive left my lips.

My husband's response was, "Bankruptcy is not the answer. Not swearing is the answer."

Well, if that attitude didn't just make me want to let a rip a stream of vitriolic bile, I don't know what did! And please note, people capable of correctly using the word "vitriolic" in context are, in fact, not stupid. Take that, you judgmental harpies! I'm a logophile. I love words, all words, especially juicy creative ones that some find offensive.

I went into a bit of a funk as I cleaned up my act. I felt less inspired with my new streamline vocabulary. I was lonely.

My husband could not believe I was having such a hard time letting go. Occasionally, I'd snap and scream, "What in the fudge do you want from me? This shoot is hard to forget! I love to goose down swear! I love it, do you hear me?" Of course I didn't really say fudge, shoot or goose down, but I'm sure you guessed that already.

After another child and many months of not being able to fully wean myself, my husband and I came to an agreement. I could not swear while the children were conscious. That seemed like a compromise I could work with. All I had to do was make it through the day, depositing my invectives into an imaginary account as I went. Then, when the kids went to sleep I could set them free onto the world! Deal. We shook on it.

My children are now five and seven and the worst word they've ever heard me say is hell, and I didn't even pull that one out until last year. I amaze myself. Granted, most adults who know me have heard me say much worse, but the precious beings placed in my care to raise and nurture, have no idea the kind of verbal exchange I'm capable of. And as hard as it is for me to admit, I think that's probably for the best.

You Have to Go Potty Now?

Potty training at Costco is a nightmare, a full blown mare of the night. It would test the patience of a saint. Truthfully, Mother Teresa would have been all, "Fudge this shoot, go in your pants!" I tried that approach again and again, but you know what? Toddlers who are potty training don't want to go in their pants. They've got it in their little heads that pottying in their pants is counterproductive to the whole "potty training" concept. Grrrrrr.

And the thing with Costco bathrooms is they're always three-and-a-half football fields away from where you're shopping. Always. So what do you do? You run like the rabid hounds of hell are nipping at your heels to get your little trainer on a potty, STAT!

Does this always work? No, no it does not. Sometimes your little one only has the strength to hold it for two football fields. Luckily, this usually isn't a problem if they're wearing training pants. Yet once they've reached the point where they refuse to wear training pants, then it's a horse of a different color. It now means finding someone to mop up the mess, dragging your disappointed and sobbing child into the bathroom to clean them up, and then returning to your shopping, damp and slightly odiferous from your recent excursion.

I managed to shop at Costco and get not only one, but two children potty trained. It was the longest twenty years of my life. Even once both girls were fully toilet trained, they still had an other-worldly obsession with the Costco bathroom. We averaged three visits every single trip: once when we first got there, once during the middle of shopping, and then again right before we left. The thing is they didn't always go to the bathroom while they were in there. But they always, always yodeled.

My two and four-year-old daughters had discovered the perfect acoustics for their new found love of *The Sound of Music*. Sometimes they tinkled first before launching into their glass-shattering version of "The Lonely Goatherd," and sometimes they started the very nanosecond they set foot over the threshold. But either way, yodeling was on the menu.

It's impossible not to be slightly mortified when your tone deaf daughters discover a love for the yodel. But it's funny, nonetheless. It's even funnier when old women, in the stalls next to them, encourage them by stamping their feet and clapping their hands along with the unexpected serenade.

Yodeling was not the only pastime my girls had in the bathroom at Costco. Heaven forbid someone was in there doing a number two. My little darlings would convulse in fits of gagging and coughing spasms. They'd sputter, as if gasping for their last breath on earth, "Oh, Mommy, I'm going to be sick!" Insert very realistic retching noises here. "That's the worst stink in the world!"

Of course I wanted to die and tried valiantly to shush them. I would quietly explain that sometimes people did stinky things in bathrooms and that it was quite normal to do so. Inevitably though, they'd carry on the whole time we were there and the poor woman sequestered in her stall never left until after we were long gone.

Then there was the time when my older daughter was three and locked herself in one of the stalls. I called out, "Margery Annaliese, what's taking you so long?"

She didn't answer and I was losing patience so I yelled, "Margery Annaliese, get out here right now!"

Again, my daughter didn't answer, but a woman in another stall mumbled, "Excuse me?"

I ignored the stranger and demanded, "Margery Annaliese, if you don't come out right this very second, you're going into time-out as soon as we get home and we're not going to get a frozen yogurt, either!"

Nothing from my daughter, but the woman inquired, "Excuse me, are you talking to me?"

What kind of moron was she? I was so totally irritated and out of patience. I snapped, "Not unless your name is Margery Annaliese, lady!"

And very quietly, she answered, "It is."

What are the odds? I laughed so hard, I immediately forgave my willful child, apologized to the stranger who thought she was the target of my ire, and subconsciously started to yodel.

I'M NOT YOUR MOTHER!!!

There are moments when I forget that hot-burning desire to become a mommy. I forget the agony of annoyingly happy families abounding like fat flies on a fresh cow patty. I block out the trauma of multiple miscarriages and the yearning for tiny baby garments drying on the clothesline in the summer breeze. I just plain don't remember those times. Why? Because now, I *am* a mommy. I've arrived to the party a bit late, but I got here. My two little girls are smart, outgoing, and full of joy. They also **NEVER STOP TALKING.**

Don't think I can't hear you snort, "Don't be so dramatic. Of course they're quiet sometimes. They DO sleep."

Oh, yeah? Well, they TALK in their sleep! I'm not kidding. These kids are so full of chatter and commentary, a little thing like unconsciousness can't stop them. I can't even poop in quiet. I started to lock them out of the bathroom fairly young, but they just sit out there and yack at me through the locked door.

I love them. God, how I love them, with my whole heart I love them. I would jump off mountains for them (and I don't go in for that crazy adventuring crap as a rule). I'd swim a river of burning hot lava for them. I'd even give up french fries for them (not that I could imagine the strange apocalypse that would

21

require me to do so), but sometimes I just want to love them in quiet.

Before all the relentless talking started, I used to think I'd homeschool them. Not that I'm a great teacher (I'm pretty sure I'd be hard-pressed to get them through the third grade) or because I have anything against our local school system. No, I was going to homeschool them because I couldn't imagine being apart from them for that many hours in the day.

Then the persistent jabbering started. Their sheer inability to do or think anything without letting me know was staggering, "Mommy, Mommy, MommyMommyMommy!!!"

The day I screamed back, "I AM NOT YOUR MOTHER!" was the day I knew the score. They were going to school, and as soon as humanly possible. My older daughter went to preschool for two years and my youngest for two-and-a-half years. They are now both in full-day school and it's like I'm a real live human again. I can even soak in a hot tub without the inquisition in attendance. It's pure bliss.

Here's the rub though: when they're away from me, learning, socializing, and talking their little heads off, I miss them. I'll see an old picture or remember something cute they said and I want to bring them home immediately. What kind of crazy nonsense is that?

The thought of them growing up and leaving home sends a chill down my spine a forest fire couldn't warm. I'm pretty sure I'm going to go to college with them and force them to move home afterwards. We'll have to build an addition onto the house so there's enough room for their eventual spouses and children, but that's not a problem.

I'm so absolutely delighted by my progeny. I love their humor, their kindness, their sense of adventure. I love when they learn something new and can't wait to share it with me. I even love their quest for knowledge, which yes, involves them asking questions, a lot of questions. But why-oh-why-oh-why can't they just be quiet once in a while?

Dear Costco

Dear Costco, I love you and I don't pull any punches about it. Having said that, I'd like to make some suggestions for your continued success and my overall happiness. They are as follows:

1. Bring the soft pretzel back. What in the world were you thinking eighty-sixing this delight from your food court menu? The soft pretzel was the perfect snack item when I didn't want to commit to a full meal. It was comforting, salty, and well, soft. It was the food version of a warm hug. I'm not the only one that misses it, either. If it's a matter of proving that to you, just tell me how many signatures you need on the petition and I'll get it to you posthaste.

2. Please move your furniture department closer to the toilet paper. The wall of toilet paper is hands down one of my most favorite places on earth. It's impossible to feel stress, anxiety, or worry when surrounded by an entire wall of toilet paper. Toilet paper, by its nature says, "You got a mess? Don't worry, I'll clean it up." If you moved your furniture department right next to the

toilet paper, I could lay back, kick my feet up, and go to my happy place, which would calm me, and result in my staying longer and buying more stuff. Everybody wins.

3. I don't like the new trough sink in the bathroom. There, I said it. The soapy residue of hundreds of previously washed hands always seems to linger and it wigs me out. While we're on the topic of the sinks, the motion sensors don't always work right away and the water is often too hot for my little girls' hands. Personally, I like the hot water. There's little chance of germs breeding and felling my household with water that hot. But perhaps you could offer a hand sanitizer option for the heat sensitive consumer?

4. It would make me really, really happy if you'd offer the chicken Caesar salad with a no chicken option. You know, just a Caesar salad? Oh, and I'd also like a choice of dressing. I'm thinking you should start with ranch and then maybe venture into blue cheese?

5. I've gotten all of my eye exams at Costco for the last fifteen years. I've purchased all of my contact lenses and glasses with you, as well. Overall, I've been super pleased. Yet recently I had an experience with one of your eye doctors that makes me think you should have them take mandatory sensitivity training. I asked the doctor why I haven't been comfortable wearing contacts since the birth of my second daughter. I'm a lifetime contact wearer and I miss the ease of them. The doctor

informed me I've reached an age when stuff starts to dry out. He says this is a common complaint in middle-aged women. WTF? First of all, I know I'm middle-aged, but geez, way to kick a gal when she's down. Also, being middle-aged, I'm a little hormonally challenged, so for his own safety, I don't think he should be opining about my stuff drying out. Maybe you could spread the word?

6. Please stop with the giant stuffed animals. Yes, they're novel. Yes, they're exciting to look at and touch. Yes, they're a steal at only $120. But who in all that's holy has room in their house for a huge stuffed teddy bear? Not me, that's who, and I'm tired of my kids begging me for not only one, but two of these gigantic albatrosses.

7. Overall, I'm very pleased with your bakery selections. On the years I'm too lazy to bake my children's cakes for their birthday parties, I always buy them from you, and they're darn tasty. Your fresh breads are lovely and you do a mighty fine pumpkin pie. I'm just wondering if you've ever considered offering some everyday pies with booze in them? You know, like a grasshopper pie or brandy Alexander pie? Maybe a whiskey bread pudding at the holidays? I think you'd do a bang-up business if you had one boozy dessert available at all times. Please feel free to contact me to discuss this idea further.

So that's it. Seven little things you could work on. That's a pretty doable number, dontcha think? Call me anytime, I'm happy to flesh out my thoughts for you. Many thanks for your consideration and just in case you're only interested in one or two of these changes, please start with number two and four.

Your Most Devoted Customer, EVER

Can I Help You Find Your Shoe?

We all have secrets we never want our children to unearth: deep, dark, dirty truths that would leave us wanting in their eyes. But the reality is these secrets make us the people we are today. They make us interesting and, dare I say, relatably human?

I love reading authors who occasionally throw the reader a juicy bone of revelation. I cite David Sedaris and the person in his household who used to wipe his dirty butt on the brown bath towels hanging to dry. This of course left his family members wondering why their hands always smelled of crap after drying them. I laughed to the point of wet pants when I read that one!

I have a dirty little secret myself. It's certainly not a moment of pride in my life and one I hope to keep from my children for as long as possible, but I do want them to learn of it, someday. After all, children need to know their parents are fallible creatures. It helps them to relate to us on a human level and hopefully makes them more open in sharing their own journeys along the way.

It was a dark and stormy night . . . Ha! No, it wasn't. It was a beautiful fall evening at Northwestern University, circa 1988. I was visiting a guy friend who really was just a friend in hopes of running into a guy I was hoping would become more than a friend. Let's call my friend "Jeff," and my crush, "Lance."

I'd been working in Chicago that day, modeling for a JCPenney catalog, and was looking pretty gorgeous, if I do say so myself. Jeff and I met up with some other friends from high school and decided to go to a party in his dorm. I was hopeful Lance would be there.

Happy day when I spotted the object of my desire across the room! Yet my joy came to a screeching halt when I saw Lance's arm around an impossibly beautiful and tiny Asian girl. Then he kissed her, with tongue and all. Gross.

She was everything I wasn't. She was five feet tall to my six feet. She was exotic. I was your standard Midwestern fare. She went to school at Northwestern and I went to school in Chicago. All of my hopes and dreams for Lance to become my knight in shining armor came crashing down at that moment, which is why I opted to have a cocktail without eating anything first.

The combination of an empty stomach, heartbreak, and exhaustion, heightened the effects of the alcohol. After only one drink I was ready to pass out. I found Jeff and asked him whose room he'd arranged for me to spend the night in. He introduced me to the girl who had graciously offered a spare bed while her roommate was away. Within seconds I was sound asleep.

Sometime later, I woke with a very pressing need to go to the bathroom. The problem was, I was still inebriated. I couldn't recall where I was, which left me discombobulated enough not to be able to find my way out of the room to search for the lavatory. But darn, I had to tinkle something fierce. In my fuzzy state, I did the only thing that made sense and that was to pee in a shoe sitting on the floor. I filled that sucker to capacity and then I went right back to sleep.

In the morning I woke slowly, piecing together the night before. I remembered Lance and his girlfriend and I wanted to cry. But something else was knocking on my subconscious to get in. I had a vague image of doing something horrific in a shoe! I tried to pass it off as a weird hallucination, but somehow I knew it was more.

I jumped out of bed, made sure my temporary roommate was still asleep, and walked around the room for a look. There it was. A once beautiful burgundy-colored penny loafer with a shiny penny on top full of my urine. Sweet Jesus! How would I ever explain such a thing?

I hurriedly grabbed the shoe and snuck out the door. I threw the object of offense down the trash incinerator. Then I went back to sleep.

I awoke some time later to thumping and bumping sounds. I cracked my eyes a bit to see my host tearing the room apart. I came fully awake and asked, "Hey, what's up?"

"I can't find one of my new penny loafers!" she exclaimed.

"Oh, um, my goodness, how weird," I managed. "Where did you leave it?"

"I left it right here next to my other penny loafer!" she snapped.

So I did the only respectable thing I could think of; I got up and spent twenty minutes helping her look for her missing loafer. Did I feel like something you might scrape off your shoe after visiting a busy dog park? Yes, yes I did, but there was no way I could come clean and confess what had really happened. There's no way you can admit to tinkling in someone's shoe and keep your reputation intact. I couldn't even offer to buy her new penny loafers or she'd suspect I was somehow responsible.

What's the moral to this story? God knows. I just hope when my children learn of it, it will make me human enough in their eyes that they'll feel free to talk to me about anything.

Crazy Lady at Costco

My mom is a character. I've often tried to accurately describe her in prose, but have failed every time. Why is that? Because in order to fully do her justice she'd need her own book and I don't currently have the time to write her. I will though, one day. For now, suffice it say, she's one of a kind.

One day last year, Mom had to have a tooth extracted. The girls and I dropped her off at the dentist's office and picked her up after the procedure. At pickup, the doctor asked to speak with me privately and suggested I keep a close eye on her. Apparently, she was still pretty hopped up on pain medication.

He also mentioned that he prescribed two pills for her before surgery to make her a bit loopy. She took one before the procedure and still had one in her possession, in case of emergency. My mom's reaction to the medication was so extreme, the doctor asked her to hand over her spare pill. She refused, indicating she liked how it made her feel. She had plans to take the other one on another undisclosed occasion. The dentist didn't think that was a good idea so he asked me to find a way to confiscate it from her.

After a bit of a kerfuffle, I managed to situate my mother into the passenger side of the minivan. I was originally planning to take her straight home, but she needed a prescription filled at Costco before the pharmacy closed. By now, you know how much I love Costco, so this was no burden on my part.

I put my mom into one those motorized shopping carts, thinking she'd be better off sitting rather than walking in her current state. We carefully got her over to the pharmacy and found out she'd have a half-hour wait. No problem. The little girls had to go to the bathroom and I promised them they could have a hot dog for dinner. I figured that would take about a half hour.

My mom was a bit miffed, though. She'd left her book in the van. She is not a woman who waits without something to do. I promised to retrieve her reading material after taking the girls to the bathroom. Then I cautioned her to stay put.

Oh boy, either I completely underestimated her ability to sit still for five minutes or I misjudged how loaded she was. Either way, once we got back to the pharmacy with her murder mystery, neither she nor the electric cart were anywhere to be found.

I asked the pharmacist if she knew where the old lady in the motorized cart had gone. She pointed toward the center of the store to indicate her path of trajectory. I grabbed my daughters' hands and away we went! Up and down, aisle after aisle, until we finally saw her. She was gunning the scooter as fast as it would go and appeared to be heading straight for a woman handing out samples. People leapt out of her path right and left. The whole thing would have been rather comical in a movie, but in reality it was terrifying. I briefly wondered if my mom would be issued a DUI, and then I worried I'd be the one in trouble for leaving her.

Just as we were closing in, my mother altered her route and sped off in another direction, again with the people jumping out of the way. There was a near miss with a center island display full of Pirate's Booty and a couple of close calls with carts that didn't move fast enough, but ultimately we caught up with her next to the potsticker lady. My mom's a sucker for a good potsticker.

I was a bit agitated once she finally stopped and I demanded to know what in the hoo ha she thought she was doing. Then I believe I yelled, "I told you not to go anywhere!"

Nonplussed, my mother assured me she wasn't a child and was simply searching out some samples. She was hungry. Like a typical drunk driver, she had no idea she was too inebriated to be behind the wheel. In fact, the next day she had no memory the incident ever took place and rather indignantly accused me of making up stories.

When I asked her what she did with the remaining pill, she told me it was none of my business. My mom gave up social drinking years ago due to medication warnings. She never was a big drinker, but she did love an occasional Manhattan. I guess in light of her good times ending, it isn't my place to begrudge her one little happy pill, as long as she promises to stay off the road after taking it.

How Motherhood Broke Me and Turned Me Into David Sedaris

I love nothing as much as reading the words of people who write about their own particular brand of insanity. Again, I cite David Sedaris and his OCD childhood where an inadvertent crack-stepping would require a return trip to his bedroom to re-lick the light switch and start his journey over.

Or Jenny Lawson! My God, no one produces the side-splitting hilarity of taxidermy roadkill like this woman. A Pat Conroy novel is enough to make me want to move to the Deep South and let my freak flag fly. If I had a freak flag, that is, which of course I don't, or do I?

In a nutshell, becoming a mother broke me. I used to be this carefree, easy-going lover of life. While not a crazy fly-by-the-seat-of-my-pants adventurer, I was light years ahead of who I am today. Now, I'm a panic riddled, fearful ball of anxiety.

I blame postpartum depression. After the birth of both of my children I spiraled into a dark hole full of doom and gloom. Incessant walking was the only thing that lightened the load. But I had to give that up when I became convinced the neighborhood gardeners were conspiring to kidnap my daughter and sell her across the border for parts. I couldn't even take her shopping with me because I was sure the checker at Target was from another planet/alternate universe plotting to steal her away to a far off galaxy.

The postpartum depression lasted a year after each pregnancy before retreating back into its hellish hole. Yet, even though the depression is over, I still haven't returned to normal. While I no longer have full-blown panic attacks, I'm still very limited in my abilities to adventure, certain boogeymen and disaster wait around every turn.

The problem is my kids are now five and seven and are starting to wonder why we never go on vacations. I don't want them to take on my ridiculous worries, so I don't tell them the millions of things that could go wrong, from plane crashes to the more elusive possibilities of being kidnapped by a white slavery ring or getting hijacked by pirates.

I've decided to face my fears head on. Next month I'm going to an award ceremony where one of my romantic comedies is being honored. I didn't go to the other ceremonies that acknowledged the same book because they were in London and Miami, much too far away from my Oregon home. I'm going to the event in Southern California because: I lived there for eighteen years, so it's somewhat in my comfort zone, I will be with friends, and I could find a way home if disaster struck.

What disaster am I expecting, you ask? It's hard to say. But my money's on the Cascadia subduction zone giving way. Sounds nuts, right? Well, *The New Yorker* recently wrote about the probability that in the next fifty years the subduction zone will produce a devastating earthquake somewhere off the coast of the Pacific Northwest, liquefying the earth and making all main thoroughfares impassable.

Our state capital newspaper has been penning warning articles pleading with citizens to be prepared to be self-sustaining in case of such an earthquake. Of course, it could be an EMP (electro-magnetic pulse) causing electronics and cars to cease working for all eternity. I should have never read William Forstchen's book, *One Second After*. Ever.

So why am I leaving? I'm desperate not to live in fear and to hopefully regain some semblance of normalcy, and because I have a plan.

I've shipped the majority of the things I'll need for the ceremony and book signings I'll be participating in to a friend. I've done this so I can fill my extra-large suitcase with items I might need in the event I'll be walking back to Oregon, all 887.9 miles. Truthfully, I'm hoping to hitchhike or steal bicycles (horses, cows, etc.) to get me most of the way, but I'll still need survival gear.

Here's the list I have so far:

- Forty-seven jars of peanut butter (you know, for the protein)
- Tang (for the vitamin C and because it works for astronauts)
- A flame thrower (not sure how I'm going to get that on the plane . . . any ideas?)
- Q-tips—I refuse to have dirty ears in a crisis.
- Band-Aids for inevitable owies
- Lots of pain killers (see need for Band-Aids)
- Rope

- Duct tape
- A wok in case I have to stir fry some roadkill for dinner
- Moccasins, you know, cause they worked for the Indians and all

Of course in the event I take to the road on foot I will have to steal a butcher knife from the hotel kitchen so I can defend myself and cut up a squirrel for my stir fry. I will also confiscate as much bedding as possible to keep me warm at night and all the tiny bottles of shampoo I can carry. That's right—I'll be washing my hair.

My friend, Jen, is leaving the same time I am for two romantic weeks in Italy with her husband. She's not insane, but has the same kind of worries brewing in the back of her mind. I've offered her my inflatable raft and paddles in case she has to make her way back across the Atlantic, but she's not biting.

My friend, Laura, will be away with her family for two weeks in Mexico at the same time. She assures me if it hits the fan, they'll just become Mexican citizens and it will all work out.

My friend, Heidi, will be at a convention in Vegas and she's all, "I'll be in Vegas. What a way to go!"

Why am I telling you all this? For two reasons, really. First, if you see me hiking up Interstate 5 with my huge suitcase, offer me a ride, give me some energy bars, and maybe a bottle of tequila. I'll need it. Second, I'm pretty sure by writing this, throwing a fifty pound bag of salt over my shoulder, and avoiding all black cats and ladders, nothing will happen to me *this* time. Knock on wood.

The upside here is that I might now be as crazy as my favorite authors and if that isn't a silver lining, I don't know what is.

To My Darlings

It might be PMS or my allergy medication, but sometimes I feel overwhelmed by things I want to say to my little girls when they're a bit older. So here goes . . .

Dear Loves of My Life,

First off, I want you to know that being a kid isn't always easy. I will try my darndest to never tell you childhood (particularly high school) is the best time of your life. I think when parents say that, they are simply advising their children to enjoy life before they have the pressure of employment, taxes, and other mundane realities. Parents sometimes forget childhood is full of worry, stress, and insecurity. I remember though. I didn't always have an easy time as a kid.

I was the girl who handed her mom ten fingernails, meticulously chewed off, on my way out the door to kindergarten. I was the one who started ditching first grade because of some unremembered anxiety that tore away at me. On that note, should you ever require a mental health day that involves staying home in your jammies, watching TV, and eating popcorn, I'm planning on being there for you. Just so you know, you only get two of these days per school year, so book them wisely.

When you read this someday, my darlings, I will be even less cool than I currently am. This is an astonishing thought, as I am hardly the poster child for coolness now. But yes, I will get even less so as the years wane. Such is the way. I'm writing this now in hopes we can bond in a past/future kind of way, as you are SO going to look at me like I'm full of crap when I throw all the classic mom platitudes your way in the coming years.

Life is an amazing adventure! It is jam-packed with dreams, both realized and not. It's full of hope and expectation. It's riddled with mind-numbing possibility and earth-shattering sadness. There will be joy so great you think your head will blow off and sadness so deep you'll want to die. That's the truth, and through it all I will love you from the deepest part of my being. You are my babies and you are the best thing that I could ever give the world.

And now for a few choice bits of motherly wisdom.

Things that do not matter:

- Petty people who try to belittle you and make you feel less-than because you don't subscribe to their ideals.
- Designer labels and new cars
- The boy of the minute, the one you think will cause you **to die if he doesn't like you back**
- Gossip

Things that do matter:

- Treatment of others. It will pave your way in life. Be kind and patient. Be thoughtful of your words before you let them leave your mouth.

- Generosity. Even if you don't have *things* to give, you can always lend a hand or an ear.
- Gratitude. Life will give to you and take from you as long as you draw breath. Make time every day to be thankful for the gifts.
- Humility. The world doesn't owe you anything. Every accomplishment and accolade you receive is a gift. It's not your due.

My love for you is the greatest thing I can give to you. I will always have your back and I will always fight for you, even if I sometimes have to fight against you to succeed.

Be true to yourself, whoever that may be. I don't care if you're gay, straight, thin, fat or if all your clothes are tie-dyed (although I will probably try to talk you out of that one). You are mine and you are perfect!

Mommy

Why We Can't Have Another Snow Day and I Don't Mean Maybe

Ah, Christmas vacation, that wondrous break in the middle of the school year full of Santa, candy, and childhood fun! It's also a time fraught with cabin fever, sniping, and almost immediate ennui of toys that don't require total parental involvement.

This year, winter break has been particularly strenuous. My six-year-old spent the better part of November and December creating artistic masterpieces to gift to anyone and everyone she's ever met (and has yet to meet). My lovely child is so full of goodwill and affection that I want to encourage this behavior. She wraps every work of art in the largest box she can find with enough tape to circle the moon, and then she stores these parcels all over the house until some unsuspecting delivery person/neighbor/Moonie shows up at the door to receive them. Even though Christmas and Hanukkah are now past, the mountain of gifts remains and I swear, seems to be growing.

My four-year-old has decided she only wants to eat soft foods. She appears to have developed an aversion to chewing and swallowing. At first I dismissed this as an impending sore throat. Alas, her throat is neither red nor irritated and she has not developed a fever of any kind. She also won't eat more than a few bites of the foods she requests. It has become so alarming I'm hauling her to the doctor (despite the icy snow day conditions) to rule out some bizarre condition only WebMD could conjure.

Over break we also made a mini trip to the Gorge. Here in Oregon, the Mt. Hood Railway simulates the great Polar Express train journey to the North Pole—in one magical hour! Our children are the perfect ages for this adventure, so we planned a thirty-six hour getaway right before Christmas. The kids loved every overstimulating, fun-filled moment. My complete and utter devotion to them was enough to get me on the train. As a claustrophobic, misophonic, motion sick, middle-aged woman, it was nothing short of a miracle that I survived.

With a plethora of childhood funk going around, we've limited the number of adventures in hopes of keeping the kids healthy enough to return to school in a timely manner. Whenever one of them sniffled, coughed, or complained of stomach pains, I filled them with enough vitamin C and homemade chicken soup to heal the navy.

Then came the day before their return to education. They'd had enough of winter break and quite frankly, I'd had enough of them. So we dressed in triple layers and dragged them off on a hike by the river. Yes, it was in the midst of icy rain and winter weather advisory. Our six-year-old worried we might meet our end. "You know," she informed, "people die during hikes. I sure hope we don't die. We're only four and six."

The four-year-old added, "I hope we don't fall off a mountain."

I assured them we were hiking between the golf course and the river. We would not be climbing mountains and the chance of their demise was pretty slim. They packed a survival bag just in case. How two apples, four oranges, paper, crayons, and toilet paper would have saved them, I don't know. But in their little heads it was the difference between life and death.

That night we tucked them into bed early and, miracle of miracles, they fell asleep in a timely manner. Only to wake up to a snow day. I'm sure the houses three streets over heard my screams of agony when the news appeared on my Facebook feed. So there we were, iced in with no hope of external entertainment. "Dear God," I prayed, "I cannot look at one more booger under the microscope. I've played enough charades to qualify for a master's degree in miming. I'm on the edge of sanity and full of holiday cheese. I want my life back!"

No. More. Snow days.

I Would Walk 500 Miles

After three miscarriages and three years full of enough heartache and worry to fill the Grand Canyon, I'd finally become a mother. For two solid days I was overflowing with more joy than I thought humanly possible. My biggest dream had come true. I was a mother to a healthy, beautiful little girl. Then my hormones reverted back to those of a forty-year-old and the whiplash change in my outlook became palpable.

My older daughter was big and breech. This combined with the fact that I was forty was enough for my doctor to decide a C-section was the most humane way to deliver. I'm no hero, so I agreed without hesitation. Because I'd had a C-section, I stayed in the hospital for three nights following delivery instead of the standard, one, for vaginal births.

The first two days and nights were primarily spent in a haze of adoration and exhaustion. I held my baby, I nursed her, I kissed her all over, and I slept. I was full of wonder and awe that I'd played such a magical part in creating this perfect being.

Sometime during the third night, I awoke from a deep sleep in a state of blind panic. Never having suffered a panic attack before, I had no idea what was going on. The best way I can describe it is to say it felt like a dark and scary monster had crawled under my skin and had taken up residency, and it was rapidly pushing me out.

I immediately hit the call button for the nurse and demanded my baby be brought to me from the nursery. She tried to assure me my daughter was sleeping and she'd bring her in as soon as she woke.

I replied something along the lines of, "Bring her to me this very instant or I'll start screaming and wake the whole floor!"

Within two minutes, I was holding my sweet love in my arms. I calmed down a little, but was still filled with such a strange sense of doom that I didn't sleep for the rest of the night. I wouldn't put her down because I couldn't let go of the feeling something very bad was going to happen. The next day I tried to explain this to every medical person (which included the guy who brought me my meals) who came into my room that something was wrong with me. I didn't feel right. I was full of anxiety. I felt crazy.

None of them seemed to take me seriously. They suggested I was experiencing something called the baby blues and it was just my hormones readjusting to their post pregnancy state. Calling what I was feeling something as benign as the baby blues was akin to suggesting Mt. St. Helens was a nice little hill or five-alarm chili was mildly spicy.

My doctor also underplayed the severity of my feelings, claiming they were quite normal and should go away in a couple weeks. The thought of living like this for two weeks was positively unacceptable. She suggested walking might help.

So I got up, put Margery in her bassinet, and pushed her up and down the corridor. I walked and walked and walked around the halls until one of the nurses told me I'd had more than enough exercise and had to be careful with my incision. Happily, the walking seemed to help take the edge off. I wasn't anywhere near normal, but I was a little bit better.

When I got back to my room, I handed the baby to my husband and told him he was not allowed to put her down. If he needed a break he was to wake me so I could hold her. The baby was to be held at all costs.

Going home the next day was a surreal experience. Our house looked like home, but it didn't feel like it. It was like entering an alternate universe. Nothing was the same as it was before I went into the hospital. It didn't even smell the same. I was not deliriously happy. I had everything I'd ever wanted in life and I was miserable.

Neither my husband nor I had any working knowledge of postpartum depression. My doctor informed me that if things didn't get significantly better very soon, I'd need to make an appointment with a psychiatrist. She was telling me there was help, but that's not what I heard. I heard, "If you keep acting crazy, the medical world will deem you crazy." and I worried they'd take my baby away from me.

So from that point on, for nearly a full year, I did my best to try to act sane. My husband was the only one I shared anything with and even he had no idea the extent of my agony. My only reprieve came when I was walking. Much of my day was spent marching around our neighborhood. I hiked for hours on end. I trekked and tramped until the paranoia set in. Once that fresh hell arrived, I was sure every car that drove by was full of Bloods and Crypts (forget that we lived in a really nice neighborhood—

this kind of crazy knows no bounds) who were going to mistake us for drug mules and shoot us execution-style. That's when I had to give up walking the neighborhood and took up trudging up and down our driveway.

Why am I telling you this? Because God forbid you ever experience postpartum depression or have a family member or friend that does. There is help. There's medication. I feel a responsibility to share my story so others will know they aren't alone. The medical world isn't trying to take your baby from you. They're trying to help you.

Luckily, my postpartum only made me anxious, paranoid, and claustrophobic. I never had any thoughts of hurting my child or myself. But I can now understand how some women do. It's no reflection of the people they fundamentally are, it's only a reflection of the monster that's taken up residency in their heads.

The Good Mother

The definition of what it means to be a good mother changes for me as quickly as the weather in Oregon. It can be sunny, raining, hailing, and snowing all within the span of twenty minutes here. It can be bright and beautiful in the front yard and storming in the backyard. Nothing remains the same for long, much like my idea of what it takes to be good at my job.

When my babies were under six months old, my notion of being a good mother meant never letting them out of my arms. If I held them 24-7, then I was a good mother. Of course I was also an exhausted mother, which did no one any favors, especially me.

I was a good mother if I never gave my infants formula and nursed them for at least a year. Of course that's ridiculous as many babies thrive on formula. It makes you no less of a good parent if you supplement. But I became kind of addicted to nursing as it released chemicals in me that helped keep the crazies at bay, which is partially why I nursed them both for twenty months.

As my daughters became toddlers, being a good mother meant buying them a lot of cardigans. Don't even try to figure that one out. At one point they had, combined, twenty-six cardigan sweaters hanging in their closet. They came in every color, weight, and pattern imaginable. They probably wore four of them regularly and the other twenty-two just hung there to convince me of my worth.

After cardigans came tights, winter weight, spring weight, cable, and sheer, hot pink, red, white, black, and floral patterns. I bought them every time the Children's Place had them on sale, which was approximately every three days. By the time I pulled my hoarded box of tights out of the closet to count them, there were forty-eight pair, many of which they'd already outgrown.

After tights came leggings, then art supplies, pajamas, and socks. How all this *stuff* made me a good mother is beyond me. But I think it had something to do with being prepared. If I had everything my children would ever need in my possession, then I could fulfill their needs and was therefore a good mother, right?

I have all these little pie charts and graphs in my head that suggest I will have truly succeeded at my job if my children hit a slew of random landmarks by a certain time. The categories include a wide array of things like, learn to swim, become proficient at a musical instrument, get off training wheels, take dancing lessons, and execute the perfect cartwheel.

As I ponder if my children have enough colored pencils to express their creative needs, I also start to wonder what's wrong with me. Surely other parents don't overthink parenthood so much, do they?

As most of my daughters' friends don't seem to possess the sheer volume of cardigan sweaters and tights my daughters have, I can only wonder how their parents define success. I asked my friend, Alicia, what she thought it meant to be a good mother.

She answered that if her children were alive at the end of the day, she'd done her job.

Another friend said she'd given her children life; she feeds them and makes sure they're relatively clean, the rest was up to them. Why can't I have that laid-back approach to motherhood? What's wrong with me?

I always thought I'd be such a natural mother. I mean, you don't go through life with childbearing hips like mine for motherhood not to come easily. Yet every single stage has been a struggle for me, from keeping them alive long enough to be born, to postpartum depression, to making sure they have enough cardigans.

The good news is I seem to be lightening up a bit as they're coming into their own. The more they express their individual tastes and desires, the more I see them becoming their own people despite the number of sweaters they have.

I'm hopeful that in another couple of years, once a few more boxes get ticked off my chart, I'll be able to breathe a bit easier. After all, they only have twelve cardigans now and only six pair of tights each. Surely that's a sign I'm moving in the right direction. I still can't pinpoint the thing that will make me a good mother, but hopefully all this worry counts for something.

Give to Those in Need

My older daughter, Margery, decided quite young she was going to make the world a better place. One day she's roping me into amassing fifty large purses and backpacks for the homeless, filling them with food, money, and toiletries. The next she's bent on rescuing the endangered species of the world. I'm never quite sure what each day will bring, but I'm very content to help her in any way possible. I feel a large responsibility to both of my daughters to aid them in becoming the people they desire to be.

Margery insists on making posters to hang around our neighborhood. "How else can we share the plight of the leatherback sea turtle, Mom?" So we hang her homemade signs on light poles while she stops unsuspecting dog walkers to bemoan the fates of the northern sportive lemur and Siberian tiger.

She's forever planning lemonade and hot chocolate stands to raise money for the needy and she regularly goes through her toys to gather items to donate to the relief nursery. Recently, she convinced me to write a book that she and her friends could illustrate to raise money for acts of kindness. I wrote the book, the kids illustrated it, and the school PTC decides where to donate the funds.

One day, my mom and I took Margery and Hope to Costco to purchase necessary supplies and feast on very berry sundaes. As we walked around collecting our goods, I noticed a lot of people smiling at us. All I could think was that they must be amused by the little girls' fashion choices. I'd recently given them greater license in deciding their own outfits, as the struggle to bend them to my will was starting to wear me out.

Both girls rather resembled orphans out of the *Little Orphan Annie* era. Their hair hadn't been brushed very well, none of their clothes matched in the traditional sense, and they were adorned in a variety of hand-me-down costume jewelry.

As we unloaded our purchases on the conveyer belt, an older woman approached Margery and offered her a dollar. I was mortified and realized I'd better make sure my girls were a little more presentable when we left home. I tried to give the dollar back but Margery was just as determined to take it. That's when I noticed the sign she was holding up in front of her. It said, "Give to those in need."

Holy mackerel! My kid had been walking around Costco seemingly begging people for a handout. Of course she wasn't collecting for herself, she was going to find a way to get the money to someone who needed it, but that's not how it looked to everyone else.

The checkout lady recognized us and asked Margery what she was up to. My daughter shared she was collecting for those in need. Our friend at Costco offered to go through her closet at home and gather some things to donate to the cause. She and my seven-year-old set up a time to retrieve the items and off we went for our very berry sundaes.

My child's desire to make a difference in the world humbles me. She's a pure soul, free of greed and entitlement, and I'm very proud of her. One day, on my way to the store, I stopped at a red light and gave a homeless man five dollars. I couldn't wait to tell Margery about it when I picked her up from school. I was sure she would be very proud of her old mom.

When I shared my good deed with her, she looked at me and forced a smile. Then she patted my hand and managed, "Good job, Mommy. That was very nice of you. But was he the only homeless person you saw today?"

I lied and said he was because I was withering under the weight of her seven-year-old scrutiny. She would rather I give away the whole grocery budget and disperse it to every homeless person I saw, than to only give to just one.

In the summer when we have a surplus of tomatoes or apples or plums, Margery makes sure we drop them off at the soup kitchen. Every night at bed time she prays that God will help the poor and needy. She asks that they be given food, warmth, and hope. I can't imagine what great thing I've done in my life to deserve such a little girl but I'm very, very grateful she's mine.

Good Old-Fashioned Programming

I introduced my girls to the *Little House on the Prairie* books in one of my first attempts to get them to comprehend the bountiful time in which they live. After all, there's nothing like reading about total and complete deprivation to make you grateful for little things like indoor plumbing, toilet paper, and Costco. We read through *Farmer Boy* before we got lazy and started to check out the television series from the library.

I forget what a remarkably well done program *Little House* was. I was in grade school when it came out and my whole family eagerly anticipated every new episode. I'm not sure how we waited a whole week for them, but as there wasn't any other choice, we waited. Today, we have the luxury of binge watching TV shows and that's exactly what the girls and I did with *Little House*.

My daughters loved Laura and Mary on sight. So much so, they each immediately took on their identities as alter egos, so when they later reenacted the episodes they knew who they'd be. My older daughter, Margery, wanted to be Laura and my younger daughter, Hope, insisted she was Mary.

Margery demanded we call her Half-Pint and started to wear her hair in braids. Hope brushed out her tresses like Mary's, and took to walking around the house with her eyes closed and her hands out in front of her. Margery practiced turning slices of bread into fishing bait and Hope talked about one day getting her sight back.

In the backyard they would practice lighting dynamite to blow through the mountain for the railway to go through, they escaped sunken wells, and ran from tornados. They raced on their imaginary horses and played incessantly with their dog, Jack, whose stand-in was Snowball, the cat.

The girls loved Ma and Pa and were equally irritated by little sister, Carrie, just as I had been at their age. Mr. Edwards became a near and dear friend whose alcoholism eventually caused them great worry.

They often forced me to play the part of the hateful Mrs. Oleson. They insisted I berate them and throw them out of my store for trying to buy things they couldn't afford. Then they'd go into their stash of costume jewelry and tie it up in a handkerchief to surprise Mrs. Oleson. They'd saunter back into the mercantile and pretend to buy everything they could dream of, which was mostly candy and shoes. When Mrs. Oleson (me) demanded payment, they threw their handkerchief down and laughed their heads off as I (Mrs. Oleson) couldn't possibly believe the Ingalls girls were rich! The peels of hilarity were contagious. By the end we'd all be rolling around gasping for breath, wishing we could really pull such a trick on Nellie's hateful mother.

Margery and Hope spent weeks trying to invent a time machine out of blankets and teepee poles so they could take money and assorted booty back in time to Laura and Mary. They plotted and planned all the treasures they'd give to their friends to make their lives easier.

One day I overheard Margery tell Hope she'd better settle down or she would skin her alive. I immediately intervened and demanded, "Margery Annaliese, where did you learn that awful saying?"

She smiled sweetly and answered, "From *Little House on the Prairie.*"

Not too long after, they started to reenact Mr. Edward's drunken episodes and the time Albert flirted with drug addiction. Then they pretended to escape from the burning blind school only to have to bury Mary's baby. Crops failed and the whole town came down with botulism. Their new baby brother died, a friend at school died, and six hundred other people died in assorted god-awful ways. There were more funerals in our backyard that summer.

I started to wonder what the heck I'd done introducing my children to all the doom and gloom of *Little House on the Prairie.* How were a three and five-year-old going to be able to absorb all the horror of Laura and Mary's lives? But you know what? They did it like any children do. They took in what they could and left the rest to filter in as it would.

The girls were Laura and Mary that year for Halloween, full-on with bonnets, pinafores, and metal buckets for their lunches. They wore their costumes for weeks on end. I miss their brand-new infatuation with *Little House.* It's been months since they've asked me to play Mrs. Oleson, but I'm hopeful the game isn't over forever.

There's nothing like the good old-fashioned programming from my childhood. All the pain and suffering had a way of making the normal days even sweeter. If nothing else, my little girls have learned that a day free of botulism is a good day, indeed.

Ahoy, Matey!

Here's the thing with kids. No matter how many times you try to explain proper etiquette to them, they simply aren't on a fast track to learn it. They think nothing of asking why the Muslim lady in Winco is wearing a *costume* in June. In fact, they're so curious when they first see her, my six-year-old yells out, "Are you some kind of superhero?" The four-year-old contributes, "Halloween isn't until October!"

Of course, I'm mortified and try to shush my little troublemakers as I glance apologetically at the hijab-donned stranger. The truth is, I push my cart so quickly in the other direction I don't notice if she accepts my contrite look or not.

One day when my older daughter was twenty months, and my younger growing rapidly inside of me, we found ourselves in the Atlanta airport. We had just come from two weeks in Florida with my mother-in-law and extended family. I was huge and exhausted. Number Two was performing a river dance on my sciatic nerve and Number One was beginning to flirt with the wonders of turning two. All-in-all it was a hectic time.

I decided to take Margery to the bathroom before boarding the airplane, as I could barely fit in one of those minuscule water closets alone in my current condition. Halfway there she stopped dead in her tracks, right in front of a woman bent over her open suitcase. My darling daughter shouts (SHOUTS!), "Mommy, look at that lady's heiney! It's bigger than yours!"

Not only does the woman hear, but everyone around her hears, too. Margery, always a lover of an audience, noticed she had the attention of a crowd, and added, "That sure is one big heiney, Mommy!" We left titters, giggles, and one mortified woman in our wake as I dragged my daughter to the bathroom.

Trying to explain to your children which truths they're allowed to talk about openly, and which they aren't, is like trying to dismantle a mine field, in a hail storm, without a map, while on fire. If you tell them there's nothing wrong with being fat, they assume telling people they're fat is okay. Heck, shouting it in the airport is darn right free game.

My daughters are fascinated by people of different colors and ethnicities. Our lives in Oregon (with children) are nowhere near as diverse as they were when we lived in Los Angeles and New York City (before children), so the kids are more apt to comment when they see someone who looks different than they do.

Margery's first experience seeing an African-American person was in Costco. She looked at the woman behind us in line, then to me, then to the woman, and burst forth with, "Mommy, look at that woman's beautiful brown skin! Have you ever seen anything so pretty?"

Thank God she was being complimentary. I'm sure the woman was not particularly delighted to be so loudly commented upon, but still, she didn't know how badly it could have gone.

Hope has always been fascinated by people with deformities

or physical irregularities. "Look, Mommy, that man only has one leg!" or "Why does that lady have little fingers on her shoulder? Where's her arm?" Mostly, people seem to understand children will be children and mine aren't that out of the ordinary. But still, their outbursts are plenty mortifying for their mother.

One day in the Costco food court, over pepperoni pizza and lemonade, Margery and Hope were chowing down and having a very animated discussion about Tinker Bell. They'd recently become enraptured with all things Peter Pan. Tinker Bell was their hero. I wasn't listening to them too closely as I was trying to rest my ears for the ride home, but I noticed Hope's eyes go as wide as I've ever seen them. Then she declared, "Margery, look, that man's wearing an eyepatch!"

Margery looked and before I could stop her, jumped up on the bench and yelled, "It's a pirate, Hope!" Then she caught the man's eye and waved extravagantly, "Ahoy, matey!"

Not to be outdone by her older sister, Hope hopped up on her seat, punched her fist in the air, and added, "Arrrrrrrrrrrr!!"

The man smiled nicely before going back to his chicken bake. I'm only grateful he didn't have a peg leg or I'm not sure I could have kept the girls from assaulting him and begging to hear his adventures of the high seas.

Now that the girls are five and seven, they're getting a bit less obvious when they notice people of interest. They're less likely to comment on someone's physical differences and more likely to discuss their fashion choices or hair color. It can still be plenty embarrassing, but at least they seem to be moving in the right direction.

Booby, Booby, Booby!

Little girls, as a whole, are fascinated by boobs. They know they're going to get them someday and that causes a heightened curiosity about them. After all, how can they possibly go from nothing on their chests to great big globs of boobs? It's a conundrum my littles like to discuss ad nauseam.

When my older daughter, Margery, first learned to talk, she called my bra, my booby purse. This made perfect sense in her little mind because purses held stuff. My bra held my boobs, so clearly, it was a booby purse. When Hope arrived, she referred to it as my booby holder.

I nursed both girls until they were twenty months old. Breast milk was their only source of nourishment for the first five months of their lives. Boobs were kind of important to them. The only problem with nursing your children for so long is they learn how to talk before they're weaned. Hence it's no big thing for them to come unglued in the line at Costco and demand, "Booby, booby, booby!"

Now that the girls are older, they like to put on my bras. They stuff them with socks and toilet paper and then walk around the house pretending to be me. Margery will instruct, "Hope Farthington, clean up this room immediately!" Hope will roar with laughter and demand, "Brush your hair, Margery Annaliese! Hurry up, I don't have all day!"

As a child of the seventies, I used to collect the plastic eggs from my mom's L'eggs pantyhose so I could stuff my shirt with them. Of course you needed two eggs so you'd be even. If you're not old enough to remember L'eggs eggs, half was long and pointy like the top of an egg and the other half was smaller and rounder. I didn't mind being lopsided if that was my only option, but I preferred uniformity.

My girls have all kinds of boob-related questions. "Mommy, why do you take your booby holder off when you sleep?" "Mommy, why are your boobs floppy when you don't have your booby holder on?" and "Mommy, will my boobs get as big as yours?"

Both girls are so boob crazy, I bought them half camisoles this year so they could pretend to have their very own bras. Neither one of them needs anything more than an undershirt, but they wear their pretend booby holders everywhere, even to bed.

I hear them quietly discussing their favorite topic. They wonder how old they'll be before they get a booby crack, which is their term for cleavage. They comment on other women's boobs in public and regularly offer criticisms like, "I don't think that much booby crack is appropriate!" or "I don't even think that lady's wearing a booby holder! Look how saggy they are!"

Hope once asked her daddy what it was like to have man boobies. I thought my husband would have a stroke as he vehemently defended, "I don't have man boobies. I have muscles!" Which led to me explaining why the term "man boobies," is not one men appreciate.

Flash forward to one of our hundreds of trips to Costco. We'd finished purchasing all our items and decided to split a very berry sundae. We wound up sitting on the same bench with a heavyset man eating a rather large lunch. I hear Margery whisper something to Hope. I don't know what she said, but Hope responded, "I don't care what Mom says, that man has boobies!"

Margery agreed, "And they're as big as Mom's! Those are definitely man boobies, Hope."

Of course, this was all done within the hearing of the man sporting said boobies. He wasn't very pleased and glared at me and my daughters. I don't blame him. My kids can be very embarrassing creatures, but what in the heck can I do? I can't give up going to Costco and I often have to bring my kids along. Maybe, as Hope suggested, he should look into getting a booby holder of his own.

Say Goodbye to Hollywood

My husband and I never wanted to raise kids in Los Angeles. We saw too many of our friends hiring people to live their lives for them. In return, they worked crazy long hours to sustain their lifestyles. One such couple had a full-time nanny (for one child), a dog walker, house cleaners, and gardener. They hired a service to prepare their meals for the week and transport them to their door. They paid extra for their dry cleaner to pick up and deliver their clothes, and then hired an assistant to organize everyone for them. No part of this life sounded appealing to us.

Sure, you could live without as much stuff as they had, but in a land where a starter home was going for over six hundred thousand dollars, even if you went without, it still cost plenty just to keep your head above water.

Friends were putting their children's names on pre-school and elementary school waiting lists while they were still in utero. The competition to get them into a good school, in your neighborhood, was nothing short of cutthroat, and it wasn't cheap. Pre-school could cost you anywhere upwards of five to seven thousand a year and elementary school could easily double that.

It's part of the reason we delayed having a family for so long. We wanted to go as far as our careers would take us before bidding goodbye to La La Land. The problem was, we unwittingly got stuck on a hamster wheel and there seemed to be no good time to get off. Finally, age decided for us. If we were going to have a family, we had to do it right away or risk it never happening. With three miscarriages before our first daughter, and one in between children, we clearly just made our window of opportunity.

My brother, his family, and my parents relocated to Oregon some years before us, the idea being that we'd eventually join them. Even though that was the plan, it was always a hazy kind of plan. Neither my husband nor I considered what we'd do for employment in Western, rural-ish Oregon. Our careers as an actor and a model weren't exactly in high demand in the Willamette Valley.

When Margery was six months old, the San Gabriel fires burned dangerously close to our house. Ash built up to over an inch thick on cars overnight and the air quality was nearly unbreathable. My husband's father died during this time. Jimmy flew back to New York by himself for the funeral because my postpartum depression rendered me severely claustrophobic, and the thought of getting on a plane made me wild with panic.

Jimmy was afraid to leave us behind, but I promised him we'd be fine. We packed our most important documents, photos, etc. and put them in the trunk of the car in case Margery and I had to evacuate in the middle of the night. I was anything but copacetic with him leaving, but this was his dad's funeral. I had no choice but to suck it up and try to keep it together while he was gone.

When he got home we had a come to Jesus moment. What

were we doing? We didn't want to live there anymore and knew it was time to get out. So we set a plan in motion to exit our L.A. life two short months later.

We arrived in Oregon on February 1st, 2010. We were fish out of water. The first thing we needed to do was adjust to a calmer and quieter lifestyle. But how in the world would we do that? Everything seemed so foreign to us. Traffic in our new town was five cars at a stoplight. No longer was there a chance we'd die from a stress-related brain hemorrhage on the 405 during rush hour.

There were no department stores in our new town, no Nordstrom, Macy's, or Bloomingdale's. The local mall was anchored by Target and Ross, which oddly proved to be enough. We missed our favorite eateries in L.A., but soon discovered some great sustainable restaurants in our new hometown. After eighteen years of sunshine, the sheer volume of precipitation was a shock to our systems, but darn if we didn't grow to love it.

Our first three years in Oregon were a blur. We got pregnant again and lost that baby, and then we got pregnant with Hope. After another year of postpartum depression, we were just about to declare normalcy in our lives when my husband was diagnosed with stage-four tonsil cancer. His ENT suggested we pray, giving him only a forty percent chance of surviving three years.

There's nothing like cancer to make you totally and completely reevaluate what's important in life. We are now so fully at home in Oregon, we couldn't imagine living anywhere else. We have fourteen raised organic garden beds; dozens of blackberry, blueberry, and raspberry bushes; and a small orchard with apple, pear, plum, cherry, and apricot trees. We even have chickens (named after Barbie princesses) and bees.

We're teaching our little girls the fundamentals of life, like how to put a seed into the ground and grow food. We're showing them how to nurture the earth so it will nurture them back. We spend enormous amounts of time together just enjoying each other. Our lives are a world apart from what they used to be and we couldn't be more delighted.

No Test for Me

By now you know pregnancy was not a sport in which I excelled. After my second miscarriage, my doctor prescribed special progesterone suppositories that were supposed to convince the baby my uterus wasn't a hostile environment. The prescription could only be made at a special compounding pharmacy and cost as much as the new couch I would no longer be purchasing.

I was so nauseated with Margery and hurled with such abandon that I popped blood vessels in my eyes daily. I looked like I'd poured blistering hot sand directly into my peepers followed by some crushed glass and a boiling tar chaser. I took to wearing sunglasses every time I went out in public so people didn't fear I was one of the living dead in search of fresh blood.

Once you've had three miscarriages, it's pretty darn hard to get excited about a pregnancy. I was petrified until the fifteenth week, which was the longest I'd ever previously carried. From week fifteen until the baby became viable, I was cautiously optimistic. Once I knew Margery had a good shot of making it in the outside world, I really started to enjoy the whole experience.

I made my husband take endless pictures of my expanding girth and I sported a poop-eating grin in every shot. Even though

I had been a plus-size model and spent my twenty year career ranging in size from a twelve to a sixteen, I had always had an enviably flat stomach. I loved to have pictures taken of my bare belly as it began to stretch for the first time. Note of caution: If you get near my gut with a camera now, I'll stab you with a fork.

I was considered a high risk pregnancy due to my age and horrendous batting average. I received an ultrasound at every appointment, in addition to the ultrasounds the specialists performed. At one such appointment, I was urged to have an amniocentesis. I had done quite a lot of reading in my years of trying to become a mother and knew there was a chance of spontaneous miscarriage with that test. The specialist, his nurse, and the stray people he grabbed off the street to try and persuade me, all said the risk was very slight, and they highly encouraged me to get one.

My response was simply, "No," which wasn't what they wanted to hear. So I asked, "Why do you want me to have one so badly?"

The doctor replied, "So you'll know whether your child has Down syndrome, or God forbid something worse. You still have time to legally abort if that's the case."

Wait, what? My face grew red and steam spewed out of my ears a la a Looney Tunes cartoon of yore. "I'm not going to abort my child, you fudging moron! This is my fourth pregnancy and the only one that's stuck. I'm keeping my baby!"

"Yes," he intoned, "but with the chromosomal abnormalities of your last pregnancy, it would be good for you to be prepared. It might not be the humane choice for your child to continue her life."

In my head, I went on a rampage, "Kiss my butt, you low life scum! You cretinous mass of regurgitated fish guts!!" It might have gotten a little fouler than that but I'd already begun my campaign to clean up my sailor's répertoire, so let's leave it at that.

In reality, I slowly replied, "Look, others can do whatever they want. But I'm having my baby and if she has Down syndrome, so be it." Then I instructed, "You absolutely must stop harassing me, do you understand?"

He understood, to a point. The subject wasn't fully closed until I signed a load of paperwork claiming I'd been made aware of all the risks of not having the test. I'm not sure if you can tell, but I'm still steaming mad over the whole experience.

Incidentally, I'd met a woman in the doctor's office the week before, who told me she'd had an amniocentesis and the test came back positive for Down syndrome. She said she and her husband struggled with what to do. They already had two other children. Both of them needed to work to support their family. They didn't know how they could afford or cope with a special needs child. They ultimately decided to have the baby, but they both stopped enjoying the pregnancy. The day she went into labor was a solemn one. Then she delivered. And you know what? Her beautiful little boy was born perfectly normal, no genetic anomalies whatsoever. Surely that's a very rare case, but still, it gives you food for thought.

After three miscarriages, Jimmy and I decided up front to play the hand dealt us. Did we want a special needs child? It wouldn't have been our first choice. Would we have made the same decision if our first pregnancy was viable but abnormal? It's impossible to say as that wasn't our path.

By the time Hope came around, we explained our history to our new doctor and made it clear from our first appointment we would not be having an amniocentesis. I don't judge anyone else for the choices they make. We all have the right to decide what course of action is right for us. But I was bent on making my choice clear.

Not only were Margery and Hope born extremely healthy, but they're the smartest most joyful little kids you can imagine. They're full of love and promise and possibility. I cringe to think of what life would have been like without them.

Hormoaning

Question: How do you make a hormone?

Answer: Kick her in the knee.

And that, my friends, is as funny as hormones will ever get. Hormones start screwing you over before you can appreciate how lovely it is not to have them. One day you're obliviously playing baby dolls with your friends, enjoying the carefree moments of childhood, and the next, you're breaking out like a volcanic eruption and sobbing uncontrollably. Of course that only lasts for forty years or so.

When I was in my late twenties, I experienced some kind of crazy hormonal imbalance that caused my hair to fall out (not all of it, thank God), and the skin above my upper lip to develop a dark pigmentation that bore a striking resemblance to Hitler's mustache. Not pretty in either case.

Hormones can cause your menstrual cycles to run amok, your immune system to fail, and your mood to swing dangerously out of control. You can even use a hormonal imbalance as a successful murder defense. (Of course, I'm not recommending this. You're better off not killing anyone.) But, that's how powerful a force hormones are in the human body.

I have two little girls who already run towards the dramatic in temperament. I'm in my late forties. If my calculations prove correct, I will be nearing/entering menopause as the girls start menstruating. I cannot tell you the terror this evokes in me.

Three years ago my husband built a shed in the backyard. It's quite a good size and has shelves wide enough to use as bunk beds. He's planning ahead, you see. The way he figures it, once the you-know-what hits the fan, he and Snowball, the cat, are going to move out there until the girls leave for college and I complete my transition into old womanhood. He figures he can lock himself in and escape the hormonal ravages sure to take over our house like a category five hurricane.

Well, he's shoot out of luck, if you ask me. I plan on fighting him for the shed. I'm fairly certain I'll win, too. There's no way I can go through the thrill ride of multiple pregnancies, two years of postpartum depression, and menopause only to be the sole target of two hormonal adolescents. Not going to happen, my friend. I can't sneeze, cough or laugh without wetting my pants. My once-flat stomach has formed a sort of marsupial pouch and my boobs appear to be growing out of my belly button. There will be retribution!

I'm not saying men have it easier. No, wait, that's exactly what I'm saying! What's the worst thing men go through? They get a little aggressive and angry during puberty, big deal. Four days a month I'm meaner and more contentious than a football team full of seventeen-year-olds. I can whip up a nasty that would bring armies to their knees.

No, sir, I'm not doing this on my own. Either we have a clear understanding that we take turns living in the shed or I'm going to stage a coup. That shed is Switzerland for both of us.

As I'm writing this, it occurs to me that maybe we just move the girls into the shed. We can use it as a bargaining chip. You want to keep living in the house with electricity and running water? Here are the guidelines:

- All emotional outbursts must occur in the privacy of your room, with no parent in attendance.
- No fighting with your sister.
- No sarcasm, ever.
- If you're late for your curfew, even once, it's the shed for you!
- No boyfriends until you're thirty.
- No tattoos.
- You may pierce nothing but your ears while living under my roof.
- You must maintain at least a B average at all time. Although now that we have this crazy core system, I'm going to have to figure out how that translates.
- You must keep your room and bathroom in semi-decent shape at all times.
- You must wash all of your own clothes, all the dishes, and clean the house.

Am I missing anything? I'm sure I'll come up with another forty items by D-day, but this seems like a good place to start. In the meantime, to quote a favorite Facebook meme, I'm either going out for ice cream or to commit a felony, I'll decide in the car.

It's a Magical World

We try hard not to discourage our children from believing in magic. In addition to Santa Claus, the tooth fairy, and Easter bunny, they believe in mermaids, unicorns, fairies, leprechauns, aliens, and ghosts. Some think this is all nonsense and some even think it's sacrilegious. Everyone's entitled to their opinion.

My parents both grew up in church-going households and raised us the same way. They were open-minded people, but didn't find themselves spending copious amounts of time reflecting on the possibility of things outside their daily scope. Until they bought their first house in Chicago, that is.

I was four and my brother was six when we moved into our two-story, ivy-covered, red brick house in the Beverly area of Chicago's Southside. The community was predominantly Irish Catholic. The homes in our neighborhood were largely built in the first part of the twentieth century and all bore all the trademark charm of that time.

We loved our house but it soon became clear we weren't the only inhabitants. Two spirits quickly became known to us. The first referred to herself as Aunt Em, a.k.a. Emma Hancock, one of the house's occupants before us. She was not considered the most mentally stable character in life. According to our next door neighbor, she was known to lift her skirts and relieve herself in the side yard, should the need arise. But as odd as her behavior could be, she was still considered a perfectly nice woman. The other visitor was a young man who appeared in typical 1950's attire. He simply introduced himself as John. We don't know how his story related to the house. John used to sit in the big oak tree in the backyard and try to convince my brother we should cut it down because there was buried treasure underneath. The idea was an amusing one, but that oak was the only one large enough to hold our swing. We ultimately resisted the lure of easy money in exchange for hours of play.

Our ghostly friends were not malicious in anyway, but it was still a bit hard to adjust your thinking to accept them as real. Enough out of the ordinary instances took place that there was no other way to explain the phenomenon than to admit it existed. Little things like conversations with the entities, the piano playing itself, all the windows being open in the middle of winter, and cakes being thrown across the room weren't something you could pretend didn't happen.

My parents eventually searched out help in hopes of understanding what was occurring. Preeminent Austrian parapsychologist, Hanz Holzer, came to our house to investigate. Mr. Holzer is probably best known for his investigation of the house *The Amityville Horror* was based on. He wrote more than one hundred and twenty books on the subject of parapsychology and was a professor at the New York Institute of Technology. Mr. Holzer was able to take ultraviolet photos in different areas of our house that confirmed the presence of our otherworldly housemates.

Okay, so the ghosts were real and we hadn't, in fact, succumbed to some kind of mass insanity. Now what? My parents loved our house and didn't feel we were under any threat, so we continued to live there until my dad took a job that resulted in our leaving Chicago.

What's the point of all of this? The point is that once you're forced to accept one "mythical" thing as real, you're way more inclined to believe in others.

According to a report on NBC news, there are 8.8 billion inhabitable earth-sized planets in the Milky Way galaxy alone. All of these planets exist within what scientists refer to as the Goldilocks zone, not too hot and not too cold. Scientists, using data collected from the Hubble telescope, guesstimate there are 100-200 billion galaxies in the universe. I can't even begin to wrap my head around these numbers. It's my feeling the god who created all of this didn't make Earth the only speck of intelligent life. I mean, how absurd would that be? We're just not that smart.

So now I believe in ghosts and aliens. It's just not too far a leap to maintain an open mind about everything else. One trip to Google, researching "weird ocean creatures," is enough to make mermaids downright probable in my eyes. My Lord, that blob fish is enough to give me nightmares for life, and the yeti crab? Full body shiver.

I'm not saying unicorns and fairies exist today (of course they may) but we live on a planet that was once host to gigantic lizards. Some were over one hundred and twenty feet long and weighed in at one hundred tons. Heck, if that's possible, why are we freaking at the possibility of one little horse with a horn on its head? Absurd.

The world is a magical place, folks, and I'm going to make sure my kids are aware of its splendor. The only thing I think I've dissuaded them from believing is that pink eye is not actually a result of a visit from the "Pink Eye Fairy," but from a very real virus or bacteria in the body. Other than that, it's all ripe for believing!

Stop It, Stop It, STOP IT NOW!!!

Misophonia is defined as the hatred of specific sounds. It's a condition where certain frequencies trigger negative emotions, thoughts, or physical reactions, or if you're really lucky, all three. It's also referred to as "selective sound sensitivity syndrome" or "sound-rage."

As if I weren't interesting enough, there's now a name for one of my less-charming traits. Hi, my name is Whitney and I'm a misophonic. If you chew nuts or snap gum within a mile of me, if you talk while someone else is talking, if you emit any sound that imitates opera, screeching, or whistling, I will immediately begin to mentally dismember you. If you scream for no reason, begin to cluck like a chicken, or make repeated popping noises, your days are numbered.

You're certainly thinking how clever I was to have had children. Children NEVER make any of those noises. As a species, they're so calm and passive, so very quiet. Well, here's the thing, while bothered when my children do these things, my innate mothering instinct does not allow it to overwhelm me. Yes, I still scream, "Stop, stop, STOP IT NOW!!!" But I don't feel violent towards them like I do others. Thank God.

All my mother has to do is think about eating potato chips

for me to come unhinged. Jazz music renders me so stabby I'll leave a restaurant if they refuse to change it. I've had to demand that strangers stop whistling at Costco lest I fall victim to a rage induced stroke. It's hard work being me.

I hate bird sounds in a house. My friend, Jen, has a bird and I've told her I will never feed it for her while she's on vacation. Tweety's psychotic tooting is like a tiny little jackhammer beating away on my frontal cortex. Chicken noises, as long as they're emitted from actual chickens are fine. Don't let me hear sonar unless you have a death wish. I'd rather be water boarded than have to listen to the high-pitched beeping of a truck backing up.

My mom used to comment on how random my intolerances were. Like I could listen to Little Bear or Franklin, Wee Willy Songs, or "Jingle Bells" over and over and over again, but if she so much as considered turning on *Law and Order*, I'd lose my crap. Again, it's nature protecting the young. If it was an annoying sound that also happens to be entertaining my children, my brain would somehow filter it out. Sadly, no such reprieve for anyone else.

French scientists did experiments many years ago to help autistic people tolerate sounds that were painful for them. What they did was to locate the excruciating frequencies and then remove them from a piece of classical music. Then they'd play the altered composition for the patient. Can you guess what happened? The subject's brain began to filter out the painful sounds so they were no longer affected. How brilliant is that? What do I have to do to get those French scientists to work their voodoo on me?

My brother, who is two years older than I am, also has the same intolerance. We joke about it together because we know the other fully understands our agony. Once, pre-children, when I lived in L.A. and Ryan was in the Bay Area, he picked me up at the airport. I was in town shooting an ad for a San Francisco-based company and I was staying with him.

I also happened to be starving. I'd taken a last minute flight and missed lunch so I picked up a salad at the airport. As soon as I was situated in the passenger side of Ryan's car, I pulled out said salad and started to eat it. I was so hungry I unwittingly chomped on a crouton. My first thought was that I wasn't prepared for how annoying the sound would be inside my head. I inadvertently bit into a second one when the car swerved violently to the side of the road.

I gave my brother a side-glance because I knew what was coming. I would have done the same thing. "You must NEVER eat croutons next to me in a car, do you understand?" he pleaded. "What in God's name were you thinking? Croutons!" he spat like trying to rid himself of a fast-acting poison. "Whoever invented these things should be pecked to death by a thousand vultures!" However delicious they are, I don't disagree with him.

That's another problem with misophonia. The afflicted person is affected even if *they* make the noise. It's not quite as intolerable, but it still rankles. Scientists estimate that up to twenty percent of the human population is affected by this disorder which makes me wonder why they aren't doing more to find a solution. I don't know about you, but I feel a trip to France coming on.

I'm Sorry, What?

I have absolutely no ear for accents, none, zero, zip. Unless you have a perfectly flat, boring Midwestern accent, I'll probably ask you to repeat yourself, repeatedly. My worst nightmare is getting stuck on the phone with Microsoft. Every single one of their customer service operators seems to be Indian. I'm in no way anti-Indian, it's just that I have no idea what they're saying. A typical conversation goes something like this:

Microsoft Personnel, *Bob*: Hello Wheatknee. How can I help you, Wheatknee?

Me: Well, *Bob*, it's like this. I keep getting a notice I have a virus and I need you to check and see if that's true.

Bob: Yes, doodly doodly doodly doo, Wheatknee.

Me: Excuse me, what?

Bob: Akbar, junkdoo, doodly, remote access, alacazam, Wheatknee?

Me: Um, yes, that would be fine.

Bob: Sidhartha doodly dingly dung, Wheatknee. Okay, Wheatknee?

Me: Um, yes, sure, *Bob.*

It's excruciating. By the time all is said and done, *Bob* may have charged me seventy-five dollars or three thousand, I have no idea. All I know is he took remote access of my computer and fooled around for forty-five minutes. He may have downloaded every last file I have or stolen my PayPal password, but whatever he did, I'm just so darn happy to be off the phone with him I could dance.

Conversely, my daughters are fascinated by accents and are enthralled every time they hear one. *Fireman Sam* used to be one of their favorite programs based solely on the accents. That's not really true. It was a cute show, but the accent played a large part in their enjoyment.

My older daughter, Margery, likes to crank call me using her father's cell phone. I'll be working on the computer in the office and she'll be in my room, across the hall, pretending to be Baguette Eiffel Tower calling from France to sell me her new line of pink luggage. There are squeals of laughter from her sister and she tries to explain why, "Zis ees zee most prrrrrrrrrfect lewgage in zee vorld! You must needs have eet!" Her French is a hybrid of French, Russian, and Glasgow.

Sometimes the girls pretend to be servants calling from London. They understand I've been on the lookout for a robot maid and since robot maids haven't been invented yet, perhaps I'd like to hire them at a mere six thousand dollars an hour.

Sometimes they call and sing to me in a faux pig Latin opera. I have no idea what those calls are about. All I know is they hurt my head something fierce.

One of the agents at my old modeling agency was French. His name was Jean Claude and he was a very nice guy. But Jean Claude often got tired of my asking him to repeat the information about my bookings, so he would transfer me to Nell, whom I understood immediately. She was from Indiana.

It's not that I don't enjoy accents. I do. I find some of them very musical and often pleasant to listen to. I especially love the sound of certain languages, particularly Yiddish. It's onomatopoeia on steroids. But in my brain, most foreign tongues immediately translate into music. I just want to hum along.

The other thing accents do is make me think of food. I know that's a little off the wall, but when I'd talk to Jean Claude, I'd often think of baked brie. Chatting with my Irish friend Emma, makes me crave corned beef, and an interlude with any English person can leave me hankering for fish and chips. What's that all about?

I'm guessing it all has something to do with the crazy way my brain processes sound. I'm just hoping my little girls don't take after me. After all, someone on the premises has to take over the calls to Microsoft.

The Better to See You With

My eyesight is pretty crappy. Without my glasses I'm considered legally blind. This means if I'm sitting in the driver's side of a running car without my spectacles on and someone else runs into me, it would be considered my fault for not seeing them coming and getting out of the way.

I would love to have corrective surgery, but the thought of a stranger shooting a laser into my eyes while I'm unconscious is not something I can tolerate. What if a giant earthquake hits at that moment? What if my doctor forgets to eat breakfast and passes out, causing him/her to completely destroy my eyeball on their way to a dead faint? What if the power goes out and the job gets botched? What if, what if, what if?

The average person might consider these possibilities so minuscule as to render any concern over them obsolete. Not me. I've lived long enough, and witnessed enough to know if it can happen, it might just happen to me. So I trudge through life with my bifocals and make the best of it.

Being extremely nearsighted has become symbolic in my life. I've discovered when you look at stuff super close up you don't see the chaos around you. You can really focus on the beauty of one thing. For instance, if I look at my whole house as a big picture, and take in the various messes the little girls leave in their wake, the dirty dishes, the ketchup spilled in the refrigerator, and the pile of soiled clothes overtaking the laundry room, I begin to tremble and shake in a kind of OCD epilepsy.

But when I avoid looking at everything as a whole and concentrate on a small area, it calms me. I usually take off my glasses for this exercise because anything outside of my nine-inch focus becomes so blurred it ceases to exist. I have one super tidy corner in my office that soothes my soul like nobody's business. I've been known to sit there and appreciate how the carpet meets the molding in perfect union. I enjoy the coloring variation in the fibers and feel the smoothness of the semi-new paint job. Yes, I look like a candidate for the loony bin, but who cares? It works.

It's occurred to me that one of the reasons I love Costco so much is because it's a giant space kept incredibly orderly, unlike anywhere else in my life. Every shoe box stacks nicely on every other shoe box. All the fruit and vegetables have their own place tidily nestled side-by-side. The milk is beautifully sorted by percentages and all those containers fit together like a perfectly completed puzzle. And then there's the wall of toilet paper! Stack after stack after stack of the most miraculous invention to hit mankind!

I have only once experienced Costco close up. It was after an eye exam where the doctor dilated my eyes, gave me some disposable Stevie Wonder glasses, and sent me on my way. It was horrible. Everything was blurred, robbing me of the wonder that is my nirvana.

After my exam, I was sitting in the food court with my husband and little girls, feeling handicapped by my lack of focus.

Just as we were getting up to leave, I remembered I'd forgotten to get lemons. Jimmy said he'd take the groceries to the car and pick me up out front if I wanted to go get them. I figured I could handle the task as I knew Costco like the back of my hand. The little girls decided to stay with me in case I needed them.

In the produce department I blurrily saw a woman grab her husband's arm and exclaim, "Howard, will you look at that woman! Look how brave she is shopping at Costco, BLIND, and with two little girls!" Then she just stood back and admired me.

While the whole thing was totally funny—I mean how does she think I got to Costco being blind?—I should have said something, but the truth is I did feel handicapped by my blurry vision, so I opted to put on a show for her. I let the girls guide me like they were my seeing-eye dogs. I bumped into things before righting myself. I may or may not have rolled my head up towards the ceiling like Stevie does when he's deep into the emotion of a song. I'm not going to say because I fear you'll judge me.

That was the only time I've let them dilate my eyes at Costco. I simply hated being in the one place I could enjoy as a whole and not be able to see it.

Calling a Spade a Spade

I grew up in a household where girl parts were called vaginas, boy parts were called penises and pooping was called a bowel movement. My parents believed in calling a spade a spade. There was no mystical voodoo surrounding these perfectly natural parts of life.

Imagine my surprise when I met and married my husband, only to learn these ordinary words were taboo to him. In his puritanical Victorian thinking, girl parts were girl parts, boy parts were boy parts, and pooping was ding ding. No, I'm not kidding.

When we had children, I was unyielding that our daughters learn the proper terms for both body parts and functions. He was equally adamant they hear some watered-down version of the truth. After much heated discussion, I finally agreed to let him have his way, but only while the girls were very young. As questions arose and curiosity developed, I vowed to arm them with the correct scientific words. A sort of truce was called.

During the potty-training years, Margery came up with her own terminology. She pottied out of her front door and pooped out of her back door. This jargon stuck in our household. I recently had a discussion with both girls where I introduced the correct terms for their female bits. Both were pretty nonchalant about the whole thing. They didn't have any questions so we seamlessly moved on to watching a show on the mating rituals of seahorses.

I hope to always be open and honest with my children, even if they venture into uncomfortable territory. From my recollection, seventh grade seemed to be the age I hit my mom with all kinds of forthright queries. For instance at the lunch table, the boys began throwing around the word, "dildo," like it was the best word they'd ever heard.

When I got home from school one day, I asked my mom what a dildo was. Without a blink, raised eyebrow, or demand to know where I'd heard such a filthy word, she seamlessly responded, "A dildo is a fake penis, honey."

Wow, awkward. I dropped the subject right then and there. While I wanted to know more, like, what in the heck do you do with a fake penis? Who thought up such a crazy idea? And where in the world would you buy something like this? It felt like a change of subject was the best course of action.

Not too long afterwards, I asked her about the word douche. It seemed when the boys weren't calling each other dildos, they were busy referring to each other as douches. My mom's explanation that a douche was a female hygiene product, did very little to enlighten me on the reason this term was being bandied about so often and apparently, incorrectly.

A couple months later, I inquired what it felt like to have an orgasm. My mom thought for a minute before responding, "It's like having an itch and getting it good and scratched." Needless to say, I scratched my arm bloody that year and just didn't get what the big deal was.

I hope I can be as cool and informative as my mom was. I mean, no one wants to talk to their children about this stuff, but what an honor if your kids are comfortable enough with you to ask you anything.

Margery and Hope's cousin, Nikki, introduced them to the word "wiener" last summer. OMG, they took to it with such wild abandon I had to threaten them daily with, "If I hear the word *wiener* one more time, I'm going to take away sweets for the entire summer! NO MORE WIENERS!"

Then the son of one of my friends lost his swimming trunks at the pool. This was the girls' first sight of a boy's business and a slew of conversation ensued. Margery demanded to know why that "little bit of stuff" on the front of a boy was called a wiener. She insisted on knowing where the term came from. I did my best to explain.

I'm not looking forward to all the uncomfortable dialogue ahead, but I darn well plan on having it. After all, nothing can be as bad as the summer of the wiener.

Pick Up Your Room!

I've just spent the last seventy-four minutes yelling at the littles to pick up ALL the Legos littering the floor of their bedroom. I've developed a pounding headache and burst a blood vessel in the eye that hasn't started twitching. I freaking loathe Legos. All those tiny little pieces of hard plastic hell, just begging to be sucked up in the vacuum cleaner, are my nemesis. They are the kryptonite to every last one of my mom superpowers.

You might have discerned that I'm not a Lego person. It's not just Legos, though. I've never been a keen appreciator of any of the childhood building materials. I didn't groove on Lincoln Logs, Tinker Toys, or Erector sets. I've also never met a puzzle I didn't want to burn. But just because I failed at childhood doesn't mean I want my kids to, so I equip them with all the enrichment junk that was lost on me. You know, for their brain development and all.

While they fight their sisterly war over, "You haven't picked up as many Legos as I have!" and "I'm gonna tell Mom you wouldn't let me help build the dungeon!" I fantasize about how amazing it would be to live in a Lego-free world. You can't even go to the movies anymore without finding out they're taking over the big screen! It's like they're on a mission to hijack everything I love. Well, so far just my kids and the movies, but surely world domination is next.

I hear Margery and Hope making sounds like they're getting ready to leave their room, so I yell out, "Are all the Legos picked up?" They respond with inarticulate grunting noises, so I further inquire, "If I come in there will I think your room is clean?"

Hope optimistically responds, "Maybe."

All I want to do is keep lying on my bed watching *House Hunters Renovations*. I don't want to actually haul my bronchitis-riddled, dog-weary self out of bed to check on their progress because it can only mean more irritation. More arguments over so-and-so didn't do such-and-such and wah, wah, wah, wah, wah, wah, wah . . . cause let's face it, that's what it all starts to sound like after seventy-four minutes of aggravation.

So I ask, "Hope, if my glasses are on and my eyes are open when I come in there, will I think your room looks picked up?"

Margery excitedly interjects, "Tell her not to wear her glasses!"

That's it. I throw the covers back, hit pause just as some sledge hammer-wielding mama is about to take out her hostility on the bathroom tile, and drag my sorry can across the hall to make noises that will render my children mute with awe.

When I get there, full-on ready to lambaste them with the full force of my annoyance, they greet me with an exuberant, "Surprise!" Their room is spotless and they're already dressed for bed without any additional threats on my part. Why do they need to toy with me? What's the payoff for them?

But then I look at their two happy little faces and realize the payoff is my surprise and delight that they finally did what I told them to do a mere seventy-four minutes ago. God, they're cute. I let them lure me into their Lego lair and show me all the cool stuff they've been building. I let their enthusiasm wash over me and make me optimistic that their love of Legos means they'll be way better at everything than I ever was. I fantasize that their joy of building will make them brilliant mathematicians and shoo-ins for NASA's futuristic intergalactic space program. I listen to their delight as they show me each and every tiny little piece of junk I secretly want to suck up in the Hoover.

What is it with these kids? They drive you to the point of distraction, push you to the limits of sanity, and then in less than a moment's time they have you wrapped so tightly around their fingers you'd do anything for them, even play with Legos.

Dear Mom,

Wow, wow, and wow, I simply had NO idea all the drama entailed in being a mother! First off, I owe you a huge apology for ever thinking you were a slacker. You know all those nights you were too tired to do the dishes and left them until morning? I really didn't get it at the time but, boy howdy I do now. Sadly, my obsessive-compulsive need for a clean kitchen won't allow me to put this task off, but if I could, I would.

Remember how you used to get cranky and threaten us with all sorts of archaic tortures: fenestration (throwing us out of the nearest window), tar and feathering, trading us to the gypsies, pulling off by the side of the road and dropping us off? I totally get it now. Totally.

OMG, the vomit! How can I ever fully express my gratitude for nursing me through all the childhood yucks? The vomit, the diarrhea, earaches, fevers, chicken pox, mumps . . . on and on and on it goes. Successfully dealing with stuff shooting out both ends of a miserably sick child should come with a sash, tiara, and monetary award. You didn't get any of those things, and sadly, neither am I.

Props for feeding us regularly. Seriously, all kids ever do is want to eat! Not only did you make us homemade meals every night, but generally speaking, they were edible. There was that monthly liver, though. What was wrong with you crazy parents from the seventies forcing your offspring to eat liver? It's possible with enough martinis it was edible, but you were only letting us eat the olives out of your martinis, not letting us drink them.

I would have preferred way more junk food as a child and remember wishing swarms of locusts (and perhaps a pox or two) on you for telling us carob was just as good as chocolate. That's like saying ear wax is just as delicious as lemon meringue pie. Pure unadulterated lies, I tell you.

In retrospect, I suppose I even thank you for that god-awful health food store peanut butter that consumed hours of our young lives as we stirred and stirred and stirred to get all the oil mixed in. At the time, all we wanted was Skippy like normal kids or maybe even an occasional decadent jar of Goober Jelly. But I'm sure we were better off with the healthy stuff, so thanks.

Thank you for all the homemade bread. It wasn't the soft, squishy, nutrient-free white bread we longed for, but all those stone-ground things and sprouted stuff was surely healthier. As an adult I even prefer it and have taken on the family tradition of not letting my kids eat white bread. They're about as grateful as I was.

As an adult, I appreciate how you cared what we put in our bodies. I'm thankful you didn't let us overindulge in the bad stuff. I have fond memories of making our own yogurt and growing sprouts in the kitchen cabinet. I even have good memories of all the years spent growing organic produce in our gardens, even though at the time I hated it with the burning passion of a thousand suns.

If I ever get my hands on a time machine I'm going to hop on board, hit the button that sends me back to shag carpeting and avocado green appliances and I'm going to buy you the biggest, baddest, Manhattan in town. Then I'm going to appreciate the crap out of you right before I call child protective services. Here's where my gratitude goes a little off the skids.

What in God's name were you thinking letting us walk to

school on our own? We were only five and seven, the age of my kids now. Yes, I know there were traffic guards at all main intersections and everyone else was doing it. But to quote a lady I once knew, "If all your friends jumped off a bridge would you, too?"

And how about letting us walk out of the house in the summer months with nothing more than the warning, "Be home once the street lights come on"? Lady, that's crazy talk! Any number of heinous things could have happened to us when we were out of your sight. What in the world were you thinking?

Yes, I know it was a kinder, gentler, different world. Yes, I know the number of boogeymen per capita was much smaller, but still I have to wonder about your potentially misplaced trust in your fellow man. I trust no one, NO ONE with my children. You'll notice I don't even trust you. My God, you might let them go outside and play!

What I'm trying to say is this, aside from all the unsupervised time we spent just being children, I'm still quite grateful for all the parenting you did on my behalf. It is singularly the scariest, most unnerving, sleep-depriving occupation in the world and you mostly did a great job.

Your loving daughter,

Whitney

Order Up!

By nature, I'm a person who likes order. I like my silverware to all point in the appropriate direction and to be segregated according to use. I like the towels to be folded the same way and stacked neatly on top of one another in the linen cabinet. I like cardigans to hang next to cardigans in the closet and socks to live only in the sock drawer (or on the mounting pile in the closet waiting for their mate to return from the hinterlands).

Does this make me the queen of organization? Good heavens, no! There's crap on every surface, as far as the eye can see, but I do try. I get that having kids means never having order again. So for the sheer sanity factor, I've lowered the bar of expectation to the perfect height for mouse limbo.

The problem is that sometimes I get so bogged down by all the disorder that I just stop trying. Then I become so overwhelmed, I cease functioning entirely. I'm currently in one of those funks.

I'm not particularly bothered by the fact that we're still eating off of Christmas dishes in March or that the Christmas wreath is still on the front door. Everything else got put away the day after Epiphany (or Twelfth Night, as some refer to it) so we're good there. I'm not particularly disturbed by the fact that we haven't hung all of our pictures up again after having the interior of the house painted last summer. Pretty much everything else is done, so I can be patient.

I'm not even concerned that the mermaid/Barbie/fairy bucket in the bathroom has begun to overflow and ooze into the hallway. I can overlook an amazing amount of junk as long as I keep up on laundry, dishes, and vacuuming. The problem is I haven't been keeping up on the basics and now I don't know where to begin. I don't even think I want to begin.

Here's where it all went awry. Last month my husband found another lump on his neck. We've been through one other biopsy since the big cancer of 2012 and it was terrifying. Happily, everything turned out fine that time.

This time though, the needle biopsy was inconclusive and surgery was scheduled to remove the entire lump. That was a week ago. We're now sitting around waiting for the pathology to come back. Every day that's elapsed since surgery has rendered me less functional than the day before. Every day I accomplish less. I even started napping which is something I never do unless I'm sick with some ghastly funk.

A couple of nights ago I gave up giving my kids homemade dinners and took to feeding them takeout, which I let them eat in my bed while watching TV, while I vegetate on the floor in my office, perhaps in the fetal position. My sheets are now covered in sweet and sour chicken sauce, fortune cookie crumbs and pepperoni pizza oil. And I don't care.

There are dirty dishes sitting by the computer, shoes strewn across the house, art supplies scattered to the four winds, and mountainous globs of toothpaste and assorted cuck all over the bathroom counter. And I don't care. At some fundamental level I recognize how un-me-like this behavior is and it's unnerving.

Last year I gave up flour, rice, cereal, and potatoes in hopes of getting rid of this fun middle aged belly that's taken up residency on my midriff. I've been cheating a bit since Christmas, but haven't gone too far adrift. Yesterday, I had cereal, pancakes, leftover pizza, noodles, french fries, AND white bread with butter.

I'm afraid if we don't get the results today and we're faced with waiting through the weekend, I won't be able to claw my way out of the rubble. I've been praying, negotiating, and promising to be a better human being, if only . . .

I hate this total and complete feeling of helplessness. By nature, I'm a take-charge kind of gal. I don't sit around and wait for life to happen to me. But all I seem to be able to do this week is sit around while we wait. I can't make the worry go away for my husband. I can't pretend everything is going to be okay. I can't even do the laundry, darnit.

*** The surgeon emailed at 12:34 Saturday morning that the lump was 100% benign!

Great Big Blue Balls!

You know how kids stumble upon the most inappropriate words and phrases at an age where they're too young to know what they're saying, and you don't want to draw their attention to the fact they've said something inappropriate because you'd have to explain why it's inappropriate to begin with? Story. Of. My. Life.

Remember that fun rhyming game young humans have played since the dawn of time? I think it was first discovered in the Bible . . . Jesus, Jesus, bo Besus, banana fanna fo Fesus, me my mo Mesus, Jesus! Anyhoo, once my girls picked this up, they did it for every word they could think of. "Mommy, Mommy, bo Bommy . . . Buck, buck, bo buck, banana fanna fo . . ." You see where I'm going here?

There's no way to tell a three and five-year-old that they can say buck and muck but not fu*k. If you start down that road, they'll plague you with questions like, "Why can't I say fu*k? What does fu*k mean?" Then once they know it's taboo, they'll say it ALL the fu*king time! I can't deal with my kids using words I'm no longer allowed to enjoy, so I try to gloss over their accidental faux pas and distract them with new verses to rhyme.

The littles used to make up rhyming songs on a daily basis, inevitably using the word "dick," like a million times. Dick, dicky, dicking, dicker, dicker doo . . . it was just dick, dick, dick. I used all my superpowers to try to move them in another direction, but darn if they didn't just love the way the word sounded.

Unlike "wiener," I figured if they didn't know what "dick" was slang for, they'd eventually stop saying it. And they did, but not until our fifteen-year-old babysitter heard them say it a thousand times. I'm sure she told her mom and that accounts for some of the questioning looks I've received.

Hope has super bionic powers to pick up inappropriate song lyrics. She clearly doesn't get that talent from me as I used to have to start and stop the cassette tape a jillion times to try to make heads or tails of them, and still got them wrong like eighty percent of the time. I cite, Steely Dan's "Reelin' in the Years." I was convinced they were singing *rolling in the yeast* until one confused friend demanded to know why I kept singing the wrong words. I thought it was some retro 70's way of saying rolling in money. You know how they used to call money, "bread," and bread is made from yeast, therefore, rolling in the yeast actually meant rolling in the money? Yeah, no. Turns out I just got the lyric wrong. FYI, I later found out (like once the Internet was born) that Creedence was singing about a bad moon on the rise, not giving me directions to the nearest loo, a la, "there's a bathroom on the right."

My five-year-old very articulately and inappropriately goes around the house singing, "I'm a joker, I'm a smoker, I'm a midnight toker." When she asked me what a "toker" was, I lied and told her it was just a random rhyming word. I didn't add, but thought, much like "buck" and "fu*k."

Anyway, this is all just a build up for a family trip we took to Target when the littles were two and four. I was pushing Hope around in the cart and Margery was walking along with her dad, when the girls caught sight of the big cage of rubber balls that shows up every summer.

Here's how the conversation went down:

Margery asks, "Can we get a ball?"

Jimmy replies, "Sure, what color do you want?"

Hope, whose favorite color is blue, yells, "Blue balls! **I want blue balls!! GREAT BIG BLUE BALLS!!!**"

Jimmy and I are torn between horror that our two-year-old is screaming about blue balls in Target and adolescent giggle fits that our two-year-old is screaming about blue balls in Target. The hilarity won out as the conversation progressed.

Once Hope got her hands on her very own blue ball, she couldn't hide her delight, and kept squealing and chanting, "Blue balls, blue balls, blue balls, blue balls, blue balls . . ."

Margery had a series of inquiries that included, but was not limited to, "Should we scrub our blue balls before playing with them or after we play with them? They look filthy," and comments like, "I hope these blue balls don't pop if we play with them too hard."

The husband and I were doubled over in hysterics. We rightly received some very dirty looks that day. I mean what kind of parents allow their children to discuss blue balls in public and then laugh about it? All I can say is those innocent-eared shoppers are lucky we got out of there before we started rhyming "buck."

On the Way to Costco

One afternoon on the way to Costco, Margery and Hope were sitting in the backseat of the car, discussing the number of children they wanted when they grew up. Margery was convinced six or seven kids would be the perfect number for her. Hope thought two would be sufficient, opining that kids seemed like a lot of work—she knows of which she speaks!

Margery waxed poetic about all the help her children would be to her, cleaning the house, cooking dinners, and rubbing her feet. I'm not sure where she gets her information, but she seemed a bit startled when I suggested she start doing all those things herself.

Hope largely saw children as a pain in the backside and asked if people *had* to have them. "Was there some way to get out of it?" she wondered. I promised her there was and vowed we would discuss it when she got older.

The conversation continued into the territory of animal procreation and which animals performed the marriage ceremonies, so the aforementioned childbearing could take place. I've sort of let the littles think along the lines of, "First comes love, then comes marriage, then comes so-and-so in the baby carriage." They'll learn soon enough that marriage isn't a prerequisite to parenthood, but I think it's an okay place for them to start until they're ready for more information.

Margery proclaimed how interesting it was that the husband seahorse was the only male in the animal kingdom that carried the children. Then somehow the subject moved on to how those babies got out. I confess I wasn't paying close attention to the seahorse documentary, preferring instead to toodle around Facebook on my Kindle. So Margery informed me that the baby seahorses popped out of a hole in the daddy's tummy.

I responded along the lines of, "Huh, well good for those seahorse daddies!" Margery asked if all animals had holes in their tummies for babies to pop out of. Was that what the belly button was all about?

I explained that the belly button on humans was actually where the umbilical cord was attached to the baby so it could get oxygen and nutrients from its mother while in utero. This seemed to satisfy her belly button curiosity but still didn't answer her question. So I illuminated that mammal mommies delivered babies out of their bottoms.

Margery gasped, "You mean they poop them out?!"

"Kind of," I answered. "But they don't use their backdoor." (Margery's term for the orifice people have bowel movements out of.)

"OMG, Mom! They use their front door (urination orifice)? How would a baby ever fit out of there?"

So I enlightened her with the information that there's a middle door that's just for babies to come out of. Margery was intrigued and asked, "So dog babies come out a middle door, huh? That's pretty cool, Mom!"

I had C-sections with both girls and they've grown up with that information so I don't think it ever occurred to them how human babies got out. I pretty much figured I just told them so we moved on to the topic of naming Margery's future brood. It wasn't until we were done with our shopping and sitting down to a slice of pizza in the food court, that I learned differently.

Margery had only taken one bite of her pizza before she stopped eating and talking altogether. I commented, "I thought you were hungry. What's up?"

My sweet little darling looked up at me with real worry in her eyes and answered, "Mom, humans are mammals."

Ah, she just made the connection! "That's right, honey, they are."

Margery gulped, "That means we deliver babies out of our bottoms, doesn't it?"

"Yup. Unless of course you have giant breech babies then you can deliver then through a C-section like I did."

My oldest daughter looked totally defeated by this information. She looked like she wanted to cry. Hope, ever the concerned younger sister, asked, "Bet you don't want six or seven babies now, do ya?"

Margery shook her head, sadly and answered, "I don't think so, Hope. I'm not sure I even want one."

I assured both of my daughters that the human body was a wonderful, miraculous, and totally gross thing, and that someday they would both probably want children. They seemed dubious, but agreed to put the decision making on the back burner until they were much older.

I can honestly say I'm not looking forward to the conversation when I tell my girls how those babies get in there, but I'm sure the looks on their faces are going to be priceless!

Along for the Ride

When I was growing up people used to always tell me how pretty I was. My brother was the smart one, which left me incensed and jealous beyond belief. I didn't want to be something as benign and insipid as "pretty." I wanted to be something that mattered, something substantial, like smart.

I was diagnosed with a learning disability at a young age, which of course played into my insecurities about not being the brightest bulb in the socket. I was almost solely an auditory (or aural) learner until high school. My problem was that while I *could* read, I garnered absolutely no information from reading. It's like the words left as soon as they entered, leaving behind no knowledge whatsoever.

The problem started to reverse itself when I was in high school. But without the same reading background as everyone else, I had a lot of information to recover. By the time I was a junior and senior in high school, I was in the honor's program, which essentially took up my entire social life. I had to read *The Brothers Karamazov* four times to everyone else's once, just to get the words to stick.

Even though I graduated from high school having passed enough CLEP tests to essentially skip my freshman year of college, I still didn't think of myself as smart. So when I was approached by a modeling agent in downtown Chicago, I bit. I signed a contract that I let dictate my profession for the next twenty years.

First off, let me say I enjoyed modeling. I got to do a lot of fun things and go to a lot of great places I wouldn't have otherwise had the opportunity to experience. I met wonderful people, many of whom are still friends today. But if you ask me if I regret my career choice, I'll tell you, hands down, yes.

In my humble opinion, no one should have an occupation that's based on something as shallow as how they look. All that does is chip away at your self-confidence until you start to think stupid things like being taller, thinner, or bustier has any real value.

I should have gone to graduate school and beyond. I should have taken a whole slew of classes furthering intellectual pursuits. I should have started to think of myself as smart, even though I spent my whole upbringing being the pretty one.

My parents never spent copious time praising my looks. They were always supportive of my aptitude and choices, even though they would have both preferred that I'd chosen a vocation in accounting or Mesozoic paleontology. Yet my past career is all water under the bridge. It's done and doesn't hold a great amount of relevance in my current life. God knows, most wouldn't even look at me now and think I ever had what it took to be a model. I blame the goat hairs, gray hairs, and weird middle-aged marsupial pouch. Sigh.

My current concern is that I'm the mother of daughters. All little girls want to know they look pretty. So I tell them. But more importantly I stress that they have beautiful hearts. Or I exclaim, "Look how gorgeous you are!" then demand, "Now spell sphygmomanometer."

I want my littles to know their worth has nothing to do with how they look and everything to do with who they are. The freaky thing is that so far, both of them possess a killer innate confidence I never had. They stand tall and proud and go after life like they're the bosses of their own destinies. I can only hope they remain like that.

It's a hard to be a parent and not project your own insecurities on your children. It's a struggle to guide them, while still giving them the latitude to be their own people. My girls are still so young and have so far to go, but if they keep on the way they've started, they're going to be lightyears ahead of me and do things I could never dream of, and I'm thrilled to be along for the ride!

Bat in the Cave

For me, motherhood is about as relaxing as sticking your finger into a live socket. I never feel prepared, put together, or on top of any situation. I'm like a blowup raft that's been tossed into a class six rapid. Essentially, I'm trying not to roll over, get thrown out of the boat, or take an oar to the head. My only agenda is to get us all through the ride alive. Barring that, it's a total free-for-all.

I would like to preface this by saying I haven't always been a freak show. In fact, once upon a time, I cleaned up very nicely and knew how to conduct myself in a myriad of social situations. From movie premiers to lunch with the archbishop of Canterbury, I had my shiz together.

That ship has not only sailed, it's sunk. Ever since my dream of motherhood became realized, the only clothes I wear are Old Navy yoga pants or jeans with at least three percent Lycra; you know, so I can actually sit in them. My shirts are long john type when I just don't care, and when I do care, whatever is on sale at Macy's or Costco that will trick onlookers into thinking I'm semi-put-together. FYI, I've found that if you wear lipstick and smile really big, people don't notice your stained and wrinkled clothes as readily. All the moms in the pick-up line are now realizing why I always look so manically happy. I'm trying to dupe them.

The only time I made a real effort to look good was at the littles' christenings. Due to a wild array of circumstances, Margery didn't get baptized until she was sixteen months old. The good news is I'd lost most of the baby weight by then. The bad news is I was already pregnant with Hope. As a result I don't even remember what I wore, but I promise you, I was as respectable as I'd been since becoming a mommy.

We christened Hope much younger than Margery. So not only was I fatter, but I was super-duper extra-exhausted to boot. This is the only reason I can think of that I thought a leopard-print dress was appropriate to wear on my baby's big day. I sent my husband to Target to buy mascara, as my last tube had dried up months earlier. He came back with some mega ultra-super bionic stuff that would have made an alopecia victim resemble a llama. I just looked like a giant hooker (all 6'3" of me in heels). It was not a shining moment.

Now that I'm a mother, I've taken to doing some of my personal grooming in the car before leaving the driveway. I keep tweezers in the glove compartment to pluck those rogue chin hairs that only show up once I leave my house. I also give the old nose a check in the rearview mirror to make sure I don't have a bat hiding in the ol' cave. Sometimes, like today, I don't do the nose check until I'm half way down our street. If, like today, there's a little something lingering, I can get it taken care of before hitting any major thoroughfares.

It's been a rough cold and flu season. As a result there's been a plethora of boogage and I haven't been spared. I was having a heck of a time rooting that sucker out before I hit traffic and was two knuckles deep before I even noticed my friend's husband drive past me. Of course I waved when I saw him (by letting my knees do the steering). You see, I still had a finger stuck up my nose like I was performing an amateur lobotomy.

This, my friends, is the grace in which I've embraced motherhood. I might as well just confess it all now. I am single handedly keeping Poise pads in business. I cannot cough, sneeze, or laugh without peeing my pants. All you mothers out there telling me to just do more Kegels can keep your opinions to yourselves. My two, over-nine-pound babies, have essentially rendered me Kegel-proof. If you catch me unaware, and knock on my car door in the school parking lot, I will tinkle in my pants. If you throw a ball, Frisbee, or mitten at me and I'm not expecting it, I will wet my pants. If I even look at a trampoline, I have to change my pants.

This new me is the result of realizing the biggest dream I've ever had. And even though I may never clean up well again, even if I'm as continent as a two-year-old, and pick my nose in public, I have to say, it's totally worth it.

Martyrdom

Me: When was the last time you did laundry?

Hubby: Tuesday.

Me: Exactly! You NEVER do laundry!

Hubby: I did laundry Tuesday.

Me: When's the last time you made dinner for the kids?

Hubby: Monday.

Me: You're making my case for me! You do nothing for our children and I do everything, always, constantly!

Hubby: Honey, do you think your aunt Flo might be coming to town?

Me: OMG, you did not just go there! Why do you ALWAYS think when I confront you about something that I'm about to get my period? Why?!

Then I storm off because I have to go to the bathroom and put on a maxi-pad.

*   *   *

Me: Being a parent was easier when I was a kid, wasn't it?

My mom: How do you figure?

Me: Well, we obviously spend more time with our kids than you did. I mean, you didn't work while we were young, so we were your only job. And of course you let us run wild and free for hours on end with no supervision. You could have gone on vacation and we wouldn't have even known you were gone.

My mom: Any chance your period is due, honey?

Me: Maybe.

* * *

Me: Sweet Jesus, would you STOP snapping your gum already?!

Margery: I wasn't snapping.

Hope: I wasn't snapping.

Me: Well, someone was clearly snapping! Do I have to take gum away from you until you're eighteen? Do I, hmm?

Girls: Mom, are you feeling okay? You seem a little jumpy.

Me: (Deep breath . . .) I'm fine. No, really, I'm good.

Thank goodness they don't know about periods, yet.

* * *

Me: Could this line be any longer?

Costco checkout guy: Sorry about the wait, ma'am. The flier just came out today so we're pretty busy.

Me: There were three whole people in front of me! You could have opened another line, you know.

Costco checkout guy: (Eyeballing my order of wine, M & M's, maxi-pads and pita chips) Did you find everything you needed?

Me: Yesssssssssssssss.

Costco checkout guy: That'll be $72.96. Do you want it on the card?

Me: No, I'll pay cash. (Then I proceed to pull out my wallet, which somehow launches a tampon that hits him in the face.)

Costco checkout guy: (Big smile on his face) Ah, I get it now.

Me: Don't even think it!

*　　*　　*

Me: Oh my God, why do you leave every cabinet in the kitchen open?

My dad: Only two, honey.

Me: Why? Do you do it just to toy with me? Because you know I can't STAND when doors are left open? Is that why, old man, is it?!

My dad: (Smiles) Yup.

Me: (Bursts into tears) I can't believe it, my own father! You're supposed to be on my side!

My dad: You need some Pamprin, honey?

Me: Maybe.

I've Lived

I've lived in some pretty interesting places in my adult life and met even more fascinating people. I shudder to think about my girls ever having experiences like mine, even though they obviously shaped the person I've become and I turned out beautifully, really.

My first venture away from my family found me in a dormitory in the concrete jungle of Chicago. It was a pretty bland existence packed full of strangers and the underlying odor of fetid sweat. Everything from our food, to the laundry, to social and gym facilities were located under the same roof. Multiple buildings connected through common interior hallways, it was like living in *Logan's Run*.

The dorm experience was short lived and led to subletting an old brownstone from some Canadian hockey players. In exchange for a cheap summer crash pad, I fed their piranha and kept their marijuana plants alive, although I didn't know what kind of plants they were until the end of my tenure. All I knew is they stunk.

The following school year, I moved in with three friends in the heart of Chicago's Little Italy. Our apartment was the second floor alley unit of a three story walk-up. Dingy is the nicest thing

I can say about it. The bedrooms were smaller than most walk-in closets today and the kitchen floor was on such a slant, we had to push the table back up to its proper place at least once a week.

We ate like Italian royalty in that neighborhood, though. Daily subs from Fontano's just a half block away, the most amazing roast beef sandwiches from the Sandwich Castle around the corner, and highbrow Italian food, like Mama Sue's, just two blocks away on Taylor St. The Fontano boys flirted with all the coeds and offered extra salami in our sandwiches, although in retrospect I think perhaps this wasn't the most innocent of propositions.

On my way to class I passed a barber shop where no actual barbering ever seemed to take place. The chairs were filled with old-world Italian men who spent their days talking on various telephones, probably a bookie operation. I tried to walk by quickly and not make eye contact with anyone, lest I accidentally fall prey to the mob. This didn't stop the head guy from venturing out to make my acquaintance. His name was Tommy. He called me Prom Queen.

Tommy seemed like a nice old guy and was always curious to know if I wanted him to set me up with one of his nephews. I always politely declined. One week I went home sick with the mumps and Tommy asked one of my roommates what happened to me. The day I returned to the city, three of his nephews brought over more groceries than my roommates and I had ever had on the premises before. We felt very safe in that neighborhood, protected by our Mafia don.

I relocated to New York City when I was twenty and moved into an apartment on 106th and Central Park West. Today this is a very nice neighborhood. In 1989 it was Spanish Harlem meets Harlem Harlem, before Harlem was cool. It was on the corner of "mugged in a dark alley" and "midnight drug deal."

The tenants in our building ranged from the flamboyantly gay neighbors who wrote successful off-Broadway musicals, to Booby, the crack whore who resided one flight down. Thelma was an old African-American lady, who lived on our floor and wore a uniform of a Confederate cap and fringed, suede leather jacket. She once had the honor of singing with Count Basie's Band. She was a relic from another time.

Thelma befriended me relatively quickly and used to come over to visit with her cigarettes, beer, and gay porn. She advised me I should always polish the marble on the threshold so people would know I was a lady of consequence, then she'd crack open a brewski, light a smoke, and teach me about daisy chains.

The tenants of that building used to think Jimmy was with the NYPD. He never told them what he did so they decided he must be a cop. Even though I carried a baseball bat when I went to the laundry room in the basement, no one ever messed with me. As "the cop's girl" I was pretty safe in our hood.

When we moved to Los Angeles in 1991, our neighbors were a heck of a lot less interesting, mostly just a bunch of white-collar types plodding through life. The exceptions were the apartment managers, who were the epitome of the Ropers. They regularly got drunk and fought over their martini cart. Then there was the Chinese guy next door who liked to throw his girlfriend around. We called the police regularly, but the noise didn't end until they were evicted.

These unique experiences and people of my early adulthood

helped shaped my life. They brought great diversity into my realm. And while I want my girls to have their own singular experiences someday (I don't really) I just can't imagine trusting the world with them, like my parents did with me.

What if that old brownstone had been raided by the cops and I'd been sent up the river for the meticulous care I gave those house plants? What if the mob boss had been a brute and arranged to have me whacked for not dating his nephews? What if the homeless drunks in our laundry room didn't respect my "cop girlfriend" status and had tried to steal my baseball bat?

None of my own experiences make me feel safe about my girls ever leaving my side. Margery seems content to stay with me forever, but Hope is chomping at the bit, even at five, to get out and explore the world.

How do people survive their children growing up and leaving them? I'm looking for real answers here, so please contact me with your sage advice. I know I'm going to need it.

Weeding Watermelons on Wednesday

I try really hard not to disparage other parents. It's my feeling if you're still breathing and you're a breeder, you deserve all the breaks you can get. If you give your kids cereal for dinner every night for a month, I'm going to congratulate you for feeding them at all. If your children wear the same clothes to school every day until they're ready for the rag bin, I'll be all, "Woohoo, look at you getting them dressed! You're a rock star!" If your house gets cleaned every six months like clockwork, I'll be the first to give you a celebratory high five and a latte. I admire and respect people who bring life into this world and commit to raise said life as best they can. Parenting is not a task for the faint of heart.

Now that I've released my mission statement, I'm going to tell you what bugs the absolute crap out of me. You gals out there in your snappy active wear, sporting makeup, and tossing your shiny blown-out hair all around, you know who you are. All I want to know is this, why? Why do you do it? More importantly, how do you do it? Why go to all that effort to make me feel bad about myself when I'd like you so much more if you occasionally left your house looking like roadkill? Is that too much to ask?

Then there are those of you parental super achievers. Yes, I'm speaking of extracurricular activities. Your kids are in school all day, and then it's off to piano lessons, cello lessons, karate, dancing, dressage, and underwater basket weaving. I just want to pick up my girls, take them home, and rest. How do you have the energy to run multiple offspring all over creation? I've decided you're all on Ritalin. While probably not true, it makes me feel better to think you're a bunch of sketchy junkies, so I'm going to keep on thinking it.

During the school year, my kids come home and play after school, no lessons. Occasionally we go to the park. In the summer, they have swimming lessons four days a week for two months. That's it. No camps, no canoeing the mighty Willamette, no soccer, no advanced tree climbing for aspiring circus people. They swim, they play, the end. What do I do while they're swimming, you ask? I watch them. And it's exhausting.

While tooling around Facebook one day, I read about a woman who makes a game out of raising her ten children. Contrary to what you might think, the game is not called, "How Not to Jump off a Bridge and End it All." Ten kids. I think there's a special place in heaven for those who have three kids and still manage to put their underwear on, but ten? That's like sainthood on crack. I have no gage for such overachieving.

Anyhoo, here's how the game goes. On Monday they munch on mackerel, maraud like monkeys, muck in the mud, and mull over melanoma. On Tuesday, they toss turnips, trip over teepees, tinkle on trees and tackle tumbleweeds. Of course on Sunday, they sing silly songs, salivate over salty sweets, snap saplings and swing from the stars. Maybe this woman is the best mom in the world. Maybe she's struggling and this insane game helps her cope. Maybe, just maybe, she's stark-raving mad and ought to consider having her husband fixed. Maybe, if it was me, I'd do the fixing myself.

While I'm complaining about the bionic capabilities of others, I can't miss the opportunity to dis on the Mormons. How can I tell people are Mormon? They are the only ones whose children eat pizza at Costco with a knife and fork. It's like something from another planet. Nicely dressed, well-behaved young persons perched next to their patient parents, unapologetically saying grace, and then very politely digging into their pizza with a knife and fork; what in the actual heck is up with that?

My friend, Jen, who happens to be Mormon, laughs when I complain about her people. She swears her kids eat with the delicacy of bulimic sharks at a chum buffet. She insists they're wild and unruly like every other child on the planet. I don't buy it because every single time I see her progeny, they're either diligently practicing the piano or quietly reading a book. It's not normal.

I guess the bottom line is this: I have your back if you're having as hard of a time adjusting to parenting as I am. If you're poorly dressed and quietly sobbing into your mocha, I'll be your best friend. But if you've got all your ducks in a row and still manage to look great all the time, please steer clear of me. I can't handle your capability.

The Most Boring Women
in the World

When I was pregnant the fourth time around, my friend Kelly asked if I wanted to join her and a group of moms in our neighborhood for a daily walk. I struggled with whether or not to go as I wasn't doing a ton of socializing at the time. I was still depressed over my first, second, and third miscarriages, and was also worried that exerting myself in any way might cause me to miscarry again. Of course there was no medical evidence to support my paranoia, but I was petrified, nonetheless.

Kelly thought it would be good for me to start hanging around other moms in preparation of my promotion to their ranks. She suggested I share what I was going through and let these other ladies support me. After all, a lot of women have suffered miscarriages. I thought long and hard about her advice and only decided to take it because I was constipated and thought walking might help get things moving again.

OMG, where do I start? First of all, I think I've mentioned I've never been cool, edgy, or even moderately progressive, in any area of my life, ever. Case in point, I was the last person I knew to get a computer and every time my pager beeped (back in the days before we had cell phones) I thought I'd run over a weird sensor in the road. Yes, I know roads had never beeped before, but at the time, I wasn't used to anything around me making that noise. In case you think I'm exaggerating and have gotten better, I'm still using a flip phone in 2017. Need I say more?

At any rate, compared to these ladies, I was the grand poohbah of hep catness. I was a Vogue cover girl to their Sunday circulars; I was the Venus De Milo (when she still had all her limbs) to their pile of rocks. I was the shiz, baby!

When I first met these moms, I was keen to be liked. As a rule, I enjoyed being adored, and assumed this group would be an easy conquest. So I put on a thousand-watt smile and was ready to take them by storm. By the end of mile one, I wanted to beat my head into the nearest boulder and put myself out of my misery. These women made watching paint dry seem like the Super Bowl of excitement. They were blander than dry white toast, and the only topics they could or would talk about were child related.

I started to lag behind in hopes they would keep walking and not notice that I'd turned around and sprinted home, as though my leggings were on fire. But darn my luck, one of them slowed down with me. I had no idea what to say to her so I tried, "Didn't you just love *P. S. I Love You*? I thought it was the best movie I've seen in ages."

She tilted her head to the side and wrinkled her brow as though to decipher the language I was speaking. When she finally answered, it was to say, "I'm sorry I haven't heard of that one."

What? How could she not have heard of it? So I tried, "Hilary Swank's latest?"

She tilted her head the other way. "Oh, I think I've heard of her. Didn't she win an Academy Award for something?"

I nodded my head slowly, not sure if this woman possessed all her faculties. "Yes, yes she did. She won best actress twice, as in two times. For *Million Dollar Baby* and *Boys Don't Cry*."

"Huh," she responds. "They must have come out after I stopped going to the movies." Noting my confused expression, she continued, "You know, after I had kids."

I gasped, "What does having kids have to do with going to the movies?"

"Oh, well once you have kids it's really hard to go out and do anything. You're just so tired all the time and the kids need to be shuttled around and then there's cooking and cleaning and grocery shopping . . ." She looked more and more worn out at the end of every word of her diatribe.

All I could think was this woman must be the most incompetent person in the world. I mean, who didn't make time to go to the movies? I sped up a bit in hopes of finding someone else to talk to or just plain disappear in the midst of their mindless cluster.

I continued to walk with these gals for a few months, primarily because it helped my constipation. I'm not sure if it was the exercise or if they just scared the crap out of me literally, but it worked.

What I learned from this group of ladies was that I wasn't going to be anything like them after my baby was born. I wasn't going to let my hair go gray, talk incessantly of vomit and diarrhea. I wasn't going to prattle on endlessly about teachers and other parents. I sure as heck wasn't going to take my school pickup line complaints to the superintendent of schools. I was going to have a life.

I planned to remain interesting and involved. I vowed to always know who the vice president of the United States was, unlike the mom who asked if I could refresh her memory. As we strolled past a steep ravine, I was tempted to push her into it, if only to save her from dying of boredom just being her. Of course I would have never done it, but she was *that* excruciatingly dull.

Flash forward almost eight years. I now have two children and can honestly say, compared to me, these gals were riveting. In retrospect, they were amazingly up-to-date on current affairs, movies, hairstyles and all things vomit and poop-related. They were superstars of womanhood. They were goddesses of all things family and sparkled like a sea of diamonds. Compared to any of them, I'm just a crusty old piece of coal and I owe them all a heartfelt apology.

The Packrats

My little girls are packrats and absolutely hate when I throw away any of their precious collections. Margery will even go through the garbage to make sure none of her belongings are in there. I hear her indignant little voice accuse, "I can't believe you'd throw this away! Do you know what this is?" Then she informs me, "**THIS** is my favorite cotton ball sculpture of **ALL** time! I worked on it for hours and you just threw it away like, like, it was trash!" Huff, grumble, stomp, slam!

Clearly, I just thought it was a pile of used cotton balls that had been littering her bedroom floor for a week. I had no idea it had any artistic significance. Granted, if she's the next Picasso, I probably just callously trashed a million dollar piece of artwork, but this kid is so prolific she'll just pop out a thousand more in the next week.

Hope beads jewelry for me like she's Louis Comfort Tiffany himself, and gets mortally offended when I'm not wearing her creations. She'll sob, "I guess you just don't love me! I guess you think I'm a horrible artist!"

The girls used to collect colorful plastic BBs, shot out of the business end of the neighborhood boys' BB guns. Our street was littered with them. The littles would spend hours picking them up out of the gutter and then save every last one of them. They would lovingly rifle through their collection and scream, "We had three hundred and forty-seven BBs and now we only have nineteen! MOM, did you throw out our BBs?"

I now have to go through their stuff when they're at school and dispose of the evidence in the outside garbage cans, if my pilfering is to go undetected. When they haven't played with a particular toy for a few months, I move it into the garage. If the transfer goes unnoticed, I add it to the pile to take to St. Vinnie's.

I also have the ability to collect and hoard, but I'm sandwiched between two generations who are much more prolific at it than I am. Therefore, I regularly pitch out my stuff in hopes of setting a good example.

My mom still has the first recipe she ever clipped out of a 1957 *Good Housekeeping* magazine. It's for New York cheesecake and it's the recipe we still use to this day. She pours over recipes, copies them out of books, and cuts them out of magazines and newspapers, before storing them away like religious relics. She used to have ten banker's boxes full of the things, but has recently and very reluctantly started to let some of them go.

Truthfully, my mom would have kept every last one and paid homage to them every twelve-and-a-half years like clockwork, when she deigned to go through them. But I started pushing her to release them while she was still alive. My threat to build a bonfire with those boxes on the day she died seemed to prod her into action.

She spent weeks going through every recipe and making a decision on what she could bear to get rid of. She started with those requiring exotic spices, figuring anything calling for an

African dukkah rub, asafetida, or sumac was probably not going to happen.

Then she compartmentalized the rest by course, putting side-dishes in one folder, entrees, desserts, and hors d'oeuvres in others. She considered things like sugar content and exactly how many soufflés she'd actually made in the last fifty-five years. She painstakingly read through them, caressed them, and mentally prepared them. After two weeks of this, she proudly reported she'd thrown out one hundred and thirty-two recipes.

Much to her consternation, I did not praise her, but asked what she was planning on doing with the other eight million and ninety-two. My mom and daughters place great significance on their collections. They are meaningful to them in ways I don't understand. Old cotton balls, BBs, and recipes are apparently filling holes in their lives and nurturing them. I just can't wrap my head around it.

All I know is that I'm trying to keep us from drowning in our ever-multiplying stuff. So every garbage day, I toss out another bag or two of junk and hope they only collect half as much in the coming week. I don't throw out my mom's things, but we occasionally have a heart-to-heart chat on how many waffle irons are too many waffle irons.

I'm either going to get them turned around to my way of thinking or I'm going to throw in the towel and start a couple of gnarly collections of my own. I'm thinking of starting with shot glasses and pill box hats. I'll be sure to keep you posted on the outcome.

Judge Not

As people, we are judgers by nature. Once we form a strong opinion about something, we become bent on letting everyone know we've single-handedly solved one of the great conundrums of the universe. What we don't always remember is that no one answer is right for everyone.

I cite every single part of pregnancy, child birth, and postnatal care. Could there be more know-it-alls out there? From "Natural childbirth is the only way!" to "You're ruining your child's immune system if you don't breastfeed them, exclusively!" to "If you eat a lot of peanut butter while pregnant, your child has a greater chance of having a peanut allergy!"

What we need to do is shut our yaps unless we're directly asked for our opinion. And then let's remember, it's just an opinion. Expectant and new mothers don't need constant bombardment from every last non-mother, know-it-all mother, and veteran grandma on the planet. God knows, with the Internet and the vast volumes of books on the subjects of pregnancy and parenting, future mommies have more information available to them than ever before.

I've had friends in tears because their milk didn't come in as quickly as it should (or at all) or their baby hadn't figured out the art of latching on properly. There are copious trips to lactation specialists and other assorted breastfeeding gurus. One friend's baby kept losing weight after birth. She sobbed, "I can't give her formula! Everyone says formula is bad! I want to be a good mother!"

When in reality, not giving her formula was way worse. A late night trip to the E.R. showed her baby was only hours away from starving to death. Formula saved her life. Why can't we just be supportive of each other and not so freaking judgmental?

Lest you think I'm being all sanctimonious, I'm guilty of judging, too. Remember when Brooke Shields gave birth for the first time and went public with her battle with postpartum depression? Oh boy, I was FULL of opinions. Like, "What does she have to be depressed about? She's beautiful, rich, famous, and just gave birth to a gorgeous daughter. I wish I had so much to be miserable about!" or "I bet she's just trying to get attention by exploiting her child." If I could, I would hop on that time machine and soundly kick myself in the rear end for ever thinking those things.

My own bouts of postpartum depression were so excruciating and terrifying; I had no idea how to navigate through them. Maybe if I'd paid more attention to Ms. Shield's situation, instead of judging her, I would have realized there was help out there. Don't you love when the karmic wheel takes a turn on you? Yeah, not so much.

I wrote a much-loved and award-winning romantic comedy, *The Reinvention of Mimi Finnegan*. It was a quintessential chick-lit, very Bridget Jones Diary-esque. It was light, funny, and very relatable. It also won awards. So when I composed the sequel,

Mimi Plus Two, I continued in the humorous vein everyone loved, but also decided to give Mimi a doozer case of postpartum depression. I wrote very much from my own experience.

I received so many communications from readers demanding to know why I would do such a horrible thing to Mimi. Some suggested I didn't know what I was talking about and that postpartum depression was nothing like I had portrayed it. These ladies were mad and made every effort to make the full force of their opinions known.

Yet other women got in touch and shared their own horrible journeys through PPD. They were sure my writing came from personal experience and they were so grateful I brought light to the struggle.

If you check out the reviews of the book, you'll see it received a lot of critical acclaim from writing publications and famous authors alike. It was even a finalist in the 2016 Readers' Favorite Awards. But boy howdy, check out the reader reviews! They're positively schizophrenic. The majority of the reviews are five-star and the next highest number is one-star.

In the end, if we could all tamp down our judgments, we'd be a lot better off. Let's not give karma the opportunity to take our self-righteousness as a challenge. Take it from me, it's no fun when the going around comes around.

Growing Up Royal

I grew up in a home where it was understood my mother was queen. As children, we knew full well we lived in a monarchy, not a democracy. It was instilled in us quite young that if we wanted to make the rules, we'd have to wait until we left home and started our own dynasties.

I was sure the day I gave birth I would join my mother in her imperial circles. I longed for the moment I finally became ruler of my own realm. I dreamed of little princes and princesses kissing my ring and doing my bidding with reverence and devotion. It was a vision that got me through some of the darker parts of my procreative journey.

Sadly, the whole royal fantasy was not destined to be. First I had to be the wet nurse, charwoman, cook, and all around house elf. Once my children were old enough to honor my position, they refused to do so. Not that they were disrespectful or overtly misbehaved. Rather, they liked to view themselves as my equal, not my minions. I have no idea where I went wrong.

Hope has started speaking as though everything she says is a royal decree. "Hear this!" she announces, "I played fashion spy girls with my friends at recess!" Or "Hear this! I will have croutons on my salad, but no cheese!" I would not be surprised to hear, "Hear this! I will be lunching on the lido deck at noon!" It sounds like something straight out of Robin Hood and we laugh at least eighty-two times a day when a new proclamation is made.

Margery will often soundly ignore me when I ask her to do something. My nineteenth command to have her pile of shoes removed from the living room goes something along the lines of, "Margery Annaliese, if these shoes aren't gone immediately I'm taking away your TV privileges for a month!"

She'll respond by raising her head out of her book and staring ice daggers straight through me. "I think you're forgetting something, Mommy." Said as though I'm forgetting myself for speaking to her thusly.

I respond, "I think not, Margery. I think you're forgetting I'm the mother (queen) and you're the child (peasant). Pick up your shoes this instant!"

Not deigning to move an inch, she responds, "Not until I hear the magic word, Mommy. Let's not be rude."

Oh, for the love of God, where did these children come from? It's as though the royal birthright skipped a generation. I thought the position of ruler would be mine, based on an inherent hierarchy. Apparently, it's more of an attitude than entitlement.

The only good news I see here is that my girls will not be pushovers. They will not accept being treated disrespectfully by anyone. For them, equality *is* their birthright. Some might fear they will be disappointed by such an expectation. I fear for those who don't realize who they're dealing with and try to treat them otherwise.

The littles are currently captivated by girl superheroes. Their play is full of capes, masks, and girl power. They are warriors for good and woe to any who get in their way! They're currently begging to take karate so they can abolish evil once and for all. I'm leery of making them any more confident by training them to be lethal weapons.

I have no idea what my girls are going to be when they grow up but I can tell you this; they will be forces to be reckoned with. At this point, I see Margery taking charge by using her heart and head to achieve her means. Hope might just take out a kneecap or two to reach her goals.

As a mother, my only desire is for my children to grow up to be strong, kind, and capable. If that means I don't get to be their queen, then so be it. I'll be their champion and their cheerleader. I'll be their caretaker and their cook. But darn it, if that pile of shoes doesn't get picked up, I'm still going to take away their TV privileges!

Postpartum Prepper

I blame my postpartum depression for a lot of funky changes in my life, like my newfound trepidation of gardeners, my fear of aliens, my heightened anxiety of everything (including gardeners and aliens), and most definitely my weird prepping tendencies.

When we lived in California, we were always expecting the Big One to hit so we made sure to have two weeks' supply of food and water. We figured that would be enough before the Red Cross hopped on their loyal steads to save the day.

Now that we live in Oregon, a land much more conducive to a devastating earthquake (yeah, only found that out after we got here), my need for preparation has gotten much greater. It's also gotten much weirder. For instance, yes, while food is important, I find myself more drawn to the need for toilet paper. Logically, I know toilet paper isn't as important as food, but I can always eat weeds and slugs. But what-oh-what are we going to wipe our bottoms with if the you-know-what hits the fan? If you say leaves, it's obvious we're never going to be friends and we should break up now.

This new oddity started while I was pregnant with Hope. I started to suffer from panic attacks during my third trimester with her, instead of after delivery, like before. I attribute this to the fact that we lived in rainy Oregon instead of sunny California and I wasn't getting nearly as much exercise as I did during Margery's incubation.

I was a gestational diabetic with both girls, so regular exercise was imperative. During my pregnancy with Hope, I got my walking in at Costco. For every lap I did, I rewarded myself by stopping off to ogle the wall of toilet paper for a few minutes. I counted how many cases high they were stacked by how many cases wide and then I'd multiply the whole shebang by thirty. Don't judge me. I was under the influence of hormones.

After four laps, I rewarded myself with the cheese and pepperoni off of a slice of pizza; the carbs were off limits due to my insulin problem. I tried to walk like this at least four times a week. The rest of the time, I braved the elements and strolled up and down the hills in our neighborhood, toilet paperless. Those were lonely walks but they got the job done and still lowered my sugar levels.

All I can say is visiting a wall of toilet paper twelve times a week (three times a day, four days a week) for twenty weeks does something to a person. For a being that already reveres the value of the product, one can go positively overboard in her adoration. One might even say to an insane degree.

Now that the girls are five and seven, my husband claims we no longer have room for my addiction and isn't letting me buy any more toilet paper until we're down to one case in the garage. He claims I no longer have any medical reason to explain my compulsion and he wants his garage back. This is obviously a topic on which we don't agree, but as I'm desperately trying to make positive steps in regaining my sanity, I've reluctantly acquiesced.

I apologize to all of my friends and neighbors in advance if the Big One should strike anytime soon. I will no longer be able to barter my toilet paper for the excess of slugs in your backyard. We will all be forced to find inventive new ways to clean up after nature takes its course. Jimmy's going to be in SO much trouble!

Of course, if the worst comes to pass and there really is a shortage and some natural disaster keeps those lovely semi-trucks full of toilet paper from reaching Costco, I'm going to take ownership of that last case, and advise my husband he can find some leaves. Let's hope he remembers his Boy Scout training and can still identify poison oak.

A Trout By Any Other Name

The name you give your child is of the utmost importance. A name helps form your identity. It can aid in building confidence and character. It can even play a part in how successful you are in later life. For instance, Adolf isn't an appellation on most expectant parents' hit list for a reason.

In the late sixties, when Lisa, Michelle, and Kimberly were the most common monikers for baby girls, my parents named me Whitney. My name set me apart from my classmates and made me feel special. Oddly, I went to Sunday school with another girl named Whitney when I was five, but never met another until senior year of high school. Then Whitney Houston came along and made our name as common as chopsticks in China. Truthfully, it was a bit disappointing and I've remained moderately bitter over the whole thing ever since.

By the time I was pregnant with my girls, it seemed people were determined to outdo each other trying to find distinctive names for their children. Avas, Katlyns and Haileys were on every corner. The phenomenon was so great, celebrities started to name their kids after fruit so they would stand out from the crowd.

For our first child, my husband and I decided to go

traditional and use a combination of our grandmothers' names. So instead of naming her Avocado Genesis, or some such nonsense, we went with the more classic Margery Annaliese. By the time Hope came along, we opted for a name that was pertinent to her existence. After four miscarriages, we were no longer confident we would have another child, but we were endlessly hopeful.

When I was in my early twenties I met a woman at my friend Louisa's house, who I swear told me her name was Wall-trout (Waltraut). I laughed uproariously at my mishearing. When she gave me a questioning, if not disdainful look, I confessed, "I'm sorry, I thought you said your name was Wall-trout."

She replied, "I did."

Darn, how do you extricate yourself from such a tricky situation? So I stumbled and mumbled, "What an interesting name!"

She wasn't impressed and responded, "It's German." She didn't add, "For a fish hanging on the wall." But that's what I thought and again had a mighty hard time suppressing my amusement.

You would think Waltraut would have beaten a hasty retreat at this point, but instead she stood her ground and stared right at me. In an attempt to change the subject, I blurted out, "You know, Louisa used to be with the PLO." Then I confided, "She doesn't like to talk about it though, so please don't mention I told you."

Let me just interject that I've never been good with acronyms, and Louisa was, in fact, never with the Palestine Liberation Organization (the terrorist group from the sixties). She was with the PTL, Jim and Tammy Bakker's Praise the Lord group.

Louisa worked in faith-based non-profits for most of her adult life, not as a radical extremist.

Waltraut appeared to be horrified by this information. And really, why wouldn't she be? I'd just told her that her hostess was a retired terrorist. She asked me quite a few questions about Louisa and I happily shared everything I could think of, as I was still trying to deflect the onus from my embarrassing faux pas.

Years later, Louisa and I were talking about ridiculous names and I mentioned Waltraut. We had a good laugh at my expense before she revealed that she hadn't heard from Waltraut in years. She thought that was rather odd and asked what else the two of us talked about at her party.

I confessed that I told Waltraut she used to be with the PLO, but other than that, not much. The look on my friend's face was absolutely priceless. "You told her I was with the PLO?!"

I nodded my head. I couldn't for the life of me figure out why she was so upset. "Lou, I know you don't like people to know, but really, I was trying to dig my way out of trouble."

"Whitney, you do know what PLO stands for, don't you?" she demanded.

I replied, "Praise the something or other, right?"

"No. PTL, the group I was with, was Praise the Lord. The PLO was the terrorist group from the sixties."

Oh crap, no wonder Louisa hadn't heard from Waltraut in years. Then there was the small fact that Waltraut worked for the FBI. She must have opened an investigation on Louisa after that party. I'm sure she found her innocent of all crimes against humanity, but found her guilty of associating with insane people (me), and decided to dump her.

Do you see what happened here? If Waltraut's parents had just named her Inga or Helga or even Brunhilda, the whole outcome of that evening would have been vastly different. But no, they went with Waltraut, and a perfectly nice friendship ended as a result.

People, be careful what you name your children. Names have consequences. In my humble opinion, you should avoid naming your offspring after fish, fruit, or wildlife. Give them a chance at success and protect them from idiotic people who will unwittingly make fun of them.

That's Just My Finger

I believe I've already mentioned how prudish my husband can be. Swearing offends his delicate sensibilities, body parts are never to be discussed by their proper names, and butt cleavage is enough to make him take off running for the hills (although I'm totally with him on that one).

What I didn't know was that he has an actual fear of boobs that don't belong to me. Years ago, my brother, Ryan, and his wife, Sarah, came to visit us in California. Sarah was still nursing their son at the time. The four of us were sitting in our living room chatting when Quentin started to fuss. So Sarah picked him up, lifted her shirt and popped out a boob to feed him.

What happened next is pure physical comedy. Jimmy's eyes popped out of his head, he quickly averted his gaze, and then he sprang up like a fully wound jack-in-the-box. He shifted from side-to-side for a moment before shutting his peepers and literally running from the room.

With his eyes closed, he didn't see his course was set straight for one of dining room chairs. He was barefoot and somehow managed to hook his baby toe around the leg of the chair as he passed by. When he finally stopped to investigate the excruciating pain emanating from his appendage, he found his little piggy sticking out at a very unnatural ninety degree angle.

Ryan, Sarah, and I all just stared at him in total disbelief. Did this grown man just run from a boob? We all started to laugh at him before I got up to see if he was okay. After viewing the outcome of his flight, I suggested we go to the emergency room to get his toe set, as it was clearly broken.

My husband demurred as he was on his way out for an audition and he wasn't going to miss it for a broken toe. So he grabbed the damaged digit, pulled it out and up and taped it to the toe next to it. Then he left the house for several hours. When he returned, he pulled off his sock only to find his toe was as black as a rotten banana.

Some years later, Jimmy had his foot X-rayed for something else and the doctor asked him what happened to his baby toe. Jimmy explained, leaving Sarah's boob out of it, and told the doctor how he set the break himself. The doc was shocked as the toe had apparently broken in three places. He admiringly remarked that he wasn't sure he could have done such a good job.

While this story is a family favorite and we parade it out often, it isn't my absolute favorite. This one is. Once, when Margery was two, she opened the door to the bathroom while her daddy was relieving himself. Jimmy always locked the door when he went to the bathroom, but didn't this time because he thought everyone was still asleep.

Margery got her first glimpse of a man doing his thing at a toilet, and was surprised to find out he did it standing up. She tried to get a look at what was going on but Jimmy managed to finagle around so she didn't see much, or so he thought.

Margery gasped in excitement, "Daddy, you're standing! What are you tinkling out of?"

Now, I don't know about you, but this seems like the perfect time to inform your child that men and women have different parts. He didn't have to say he had a penis, he could have simply stated that he went potty out of his boy part. Simple, right? Of course that isn't what happened. In his horror at being caught going to the bathroom by his daughter, my husband answered, "That's just my other finger, honey."

Margery was delighted by this new information and ran off to find me so she could share that boys had more fingers than girls and they go potty out of one of them! To commemorate the event, she asked to be put in her high chair with her Play-Doh. This is where she perfectly recreated the scene of Daddy tinkling out of his finger. I took a picture to remember it by.

Thank goodness the girls have me to get their information from. Imagine if Jimmy and I were both so Victorian in our sensibilities. Our poor littles would have grown up thinking babies were dumped on your doorstep by giant birds and men piddled out of their fingers.

The Best Thing You Can Do

You know how it's said that the best thing a father can do for his children is to love their mother? This is truth. Children grow up intently watching the dynamics between their parents. What they witness, day-in and day-out during their upbringing, becomes what they search out in their own lives.

If parents fight, swear at, or belittle each other, you can bet your bottom dollar their kids will strike out into the world subconsciously looking for that which is familiar to them; if they witness love, consideration, and caring, they will settle for nothing less. The weight of doing right by the precious lives entrusted in our care is pretty intense, isn't it?

My parents were always a united force in front of us. We learned early on that we could never play them against each other, which of course was a grave disappointment, as manipulation and subterfuge are some of the first areas children explore to create the outcomes they most desire.

We grew up knowing our parents loved one another and respected one another. My mom and dad kept their disagreements behind closed doors and we rarely heard them argue. The few times they fought in our earshot, we were sure it meant divorce, as it was such a rare occurrence. Of course nobody divorces over how the toothpaste tube is squeezed, but we didn't know that.

From as early as memory allows, I remember my dad confessing that my mother was the love of his life. He says it to this day, after nearly fifty-six years of marriage. He often gets tears in his eyes when he speaks of it; such is the depth of his feeling. My father set the bar very high for the man who would one day be my husband.

My mom often says she never knew a better father than my dad. He loved to play with his children, he loved to talk with us, and share information with us. No conversation was considered too far out in left field to explore. Even though he was the dad, he was really just a big kid enjoying a second shot at childhood through his own offspring.

The carefree innocence of my dad's own youth was cut short when he was twelve and his mother died. As such, he was determined not to miss the opportunity to relive a more joyful outcome with his own kids. Ultimately, we were the beneficiaries of his loss.

My dad dropped me off at college by himself. He trusted the job he and my mom had done raising me, and he sent me off into the world with the following advice, "Remember to have fun." You'd think a parent would lecture their child to work hard and keep their nose to the grindstone, etc., reiterating all the parental platitudes we know so well. But my dad knew how hard life could be, and that there would always be work to fill my time. He wanted to make sure I invested some effort in fun. So as not to let him down, I followed his advice to the letter.

It's a thrill for me that my parents are both still alive and my children are getting to have close relationships with them. The more I delve into this parenting thing, the more I realize what incredible people my parents are. I'm now fully aware of all the sacrifices and hard work that went into creating the adult version of me.

I'm grateful beyond measure to both of my parents for the role models they were. Without their devotion to one another, I might not have demanded the same from my mate, and like my mom before me, I hit the husband jackpot.

I know Jimmy adores me (even if he takes the garbage out six minutes after I think he should) and he's devoted to our children. Most importantly though, he's showing our daughters how they should be treated.

We're doing our best raising the littles. I'm sure we'll make mistakes as we go. But one thing's a guarantee; they'll enter adulthood knowing they deserve the best by virtue of how their poppy and daddy loved their wives.

Meet the Littles

I keep a journal of some of the funny and memorable conversations with my girls. There's so much I don't want to forget and there's pretty much a french fry's chance in my mouth that I'll remember everything. Here are a few snippets of their fifth and seventh years for your enjoyment.

On her birthday:

Hope: Mommy, turning a new number is hard work.

*　　*　　*

The month after she turned five, Hope decided to start a band at the swimming pool. She started composing songs so they would have original material.

The Love Song
The sun rises at the very beginning
and fills your heart.
Where do you begin?
In your family, with your heart.

Once again, today, there's so much time to play,
and I can't stay away.
Where do you start, and where do you begin
when your heart is filled with love?

The Forever Forest

Once upon a time, there was a kingdom far away.
There was you and me to stay together,
the kingdom fire.
Softly, you can, the kingdom got broke.
The kingdom got broke.

The princess died in the fire.
How I miss everything.
But they died forever.
In the Forever Forest they got lost,
just as I expected.
There is one way to save the day.
The heart, you gotta be free!

*   *   *

Margery: Mom, Mommy, Mom, guess what? I have a joke.
Wanna know what an assassin is?(!) Mommy, Mom, I have
another joke about vomit. Wanna hear the one about poop?
Mom, what's this song about? It's making me sad, can you
turn it off? Mommy, guess what? Did you know assassins
stab people in the neck? (!!) Knock, knock . . .

And herein lies the last three hours of my life. The assassin thing makes me a little nervous.

*   *   *

Hope: Mommy, I had two HUGE pieces of salami for snack at school. Seriously, they were the size of my head!

Me: So you don't want lunch today?

Hope: No protein, Mom. My protein is filled, but my carbohydrates are totally empty!

The apple doesn't fall far from the tree.

*   *   *

Margery: Mommy, did you have frappuccinos when you were little?

Me: Nope, frappuccinos didn't exist then.

Hope: (Gasps!) Poor Mommy, they didn't even have frappuccinos in the olden days!

Margery: That must have been tough, huh?

* *#firstworldchildhoods #kidsneedtougheningup*

*   *   *

Hope: I believe in everything, even boy stuff. But I'm glad monsters are extincted, especially that three dog-headed one.

*   *   *

Me: Margery, what did you dream about?

Margery: The world, good people, happy families, and vegetation.

*   *   *

Margery: Mommy, when you're old and infirm, you know, not firm anymore, I'm gonna cook you healthy dinners.

*Ah, the seven-year-old-is trying out new words . . . incorrectly.

*   *   *

Margery: Hope, do you want me to give you a taste of your own medicine?

Hope: Yeah, medicine tastes good!

* #bubblegumflavored

*   *   *

Margery: Mommy, can I let Snowball in?

Me: Later on when it gets hot out, honey.

Margery (to Snowball): Oh, Snowball. I don't know why Mommy wants to kill you (sob).

*   *   *

Me: How was school today, girlies?

Margery: FANtastic!

Hope: Treacherous.

*The five-year-old is trying on some new words.

*   *   *

Margery: Mommy, when does the soul go into the body?

Me: I wish I knew, honey. That's a question a lot of people have. When do you think it happens?

Margery: I think life is like one of my drawings. First, I do the outline. That's like the body forming. When that's done it's time for the colors or the soul.

* Brilliant!

*   *   *

Hope: Mom, have you ever been to the 70's and 80's?

*   *   *

Margery: If I had to be any other species than human, I'd pick house cat.

* She gets that from me.

*   *   *

Margery: Mom, how do you spell "ironic"?

Me: Why?

Margery: I'm using it in my homework.

* I'm kind of wondering what a second grader thinks is ironic about her homework.

*　　*　　*

Three wildly different reviews as Wonder Woman, a.k.a. Linda Carter, runs around the beach wearing next to nothing:

Jimmy: She's a brilliant actress, isn't she?

Margery: I find the running in slow motion very exciting! It really builds the tension.

Hope: Kick 'em in the face, Wonder Woman! Rip their hair out!!!

*　　*　　*

Margery: Mom, when I grow up, I'm going to go to the gym every other couple of days or so.

*The unexpressed thought being . . . during leap year. She gets that kind of dedication from me.

*　　*　　*

Margery: Mom, when we go adventuring we need to bring rope, arrows, research books, and baking soda.

Me: Baking soda?

Margery: Use your head, Mom. We can blow baking soda into the air to see if there are invisible laser beams.

Which makes me wonder, where in the heck does she think we're going?

*　　*　　*

My mom: Margery, what are the names of the three kings?

Margery: (thinking) Melchior, Caspar and, um . . . oh yeah, Balthazar.

My mom: Very good!

Hope: Noooooooooooooooo, Elvis is king!!!

*　　*　　*

The littles have been watching a lot of cooking competitions lately. The result is the following conversation discussing the slice of peanut butter cheesecake they split at dinner.

Margery: It has a nice robust peanut butter flavor and the whipped cream is the perfect accompaniment.

Hope: But's what's up with the mint leaf garnish? Mint and peanut butter? I'd rethink that.

*　　*　　*

Margery: I'm naming my first baby Princess Esmerelda Marina Ruby.

* Which leads me to believe Margery thinks she's going to be made queen.

*　　*　　*

Hope: Mommy, we need scissors, string, balloons, and cotton balls.

Me: Of course you do.

* And another day has started.

*　　*　　*

Hope: I helped a veteran today. I colored him a picture.

Margery: Oh yeah, I wrote to a veteran and thanked him for protecting our country by joining the Continental Army.

* Methinks Margery is having some kind of past life flashback.

*　　*　　*

While watching Worst Cooks in America . . .

Margery: He might be pretty, but he sure doesn't know how to cook.

*　　*　　*

Listening to "Funky Town" in the car on the way home from Costco . . .

Margery: Mommy, they didn't use any imagination when they wrote this song. All they say is, "Won't you take me to funky town?"

Hope: It's all about the rockin' beat, Margery.

*   *   *

Margery: Mommy, I realize my homework isn't due until Thursday, but I don't like to wait until the last minute.

* If she didn't look so much like us I'd be envisioning a switched at birth scenario.

*   *   *

The girls come into the kitchen to make Uncle Ryan's birthday cake and Margery has a visible bump.

Hope: My name's Lucille and this is my aunt Martha. I'm eighteen and she's twenty-five. Let's get this show on the road cause this baby's in a hurry.

*   *   *

Listening to the girls playing Barbies:

Hope: Whatcha doin'?

Margery: Just chillin' like a villain.

*   *   *

Driving to school we pass a jogger with no shirt on.

Margery: Put your shirt on!

Hope: Nobody wants to see that!

*   *   *

Margery: Mommy, I'm here to make the world a better place. I have things to do and you have to help. Where should we start?

*   *   *

Me: Margery, Margery, Margery, Margery, Margery . . .

Margery: Mommy, stop that! It's annoying!

Me: Exactly.

*   *   *

Hope: Mommy, I love your fat legs. They're so comfortable to lay on.

Me: Um, thanks.

*   *   *

Margery: Hope, you snap, I'll clap, and Mommy, you shimmy.

* That's right, now you know how we get down with our bad selves in the car.

*　　*　　*

Three emergency vehicles passed us on the road yesterday and pulled into the parking lot of a store.

Margery: I hope everyone's okay! I wonder what happened.

Hope: It's probably that darn whiskey.

Margery: (derisively) I bet that's a saloon.

* In truth I think it was a hubcap store.

*　　*　　*

Margery: Mommy, when I grow up I'm going to have to buy another addition for the house.

Me: Why, honey? We have a lot of room.

Margery: Because I'm going to get married and have babies. We'll need the space.

Hope: Not me, I'm outta here.

*　　*　　*

About the Author

Whitney Dineen is an award-winning romantic comedy and middle reader fiction author. She lives in the Pacific Northwest with her family. In her free time, she likes to laugh, mostly at herself. Whitney loves to hear from her readers. You can reach her on her website WhitneyDineen.com, on Twitter @WhitneyDineen, and on Facebook. Sign up for her newsletter here and get a free copy of her short, *Going Up*. Also, be the first to know when she has a new release or special offers just for her fans.

If you enjoyed this book, please leave a review and help spread the word!

Turn the page for teasers from Whitney's bestselling and award-winning romantic comedy, *The Reinvention of Mimi Finnegan*, and the first in her middle reader series, *Wilhelmina and the Willamette Wig Factory*.

The Reinvention of Mimi Finnegan

Chapter 1

"A Bunion?" I shriek.

"It would appear so." answers Dr. Foster, the podiatrist referred by my HMO.

"Aren't bunions something old people get?"

"Yes," he replies. "That's normally the case, but not always. Bunions grow after years of walking incorrectly, or in some instances, not wearing the proper shoes."

Still perplexed, I ask, "What am I doing with one then? I'm only thirty-four."

He says that by the atypical location of my bunion, he can deduce I have the tendency to walk on the outsides of my feet. He explains that while some people walk on the insides of their feet, giving them a knock-kneed appearance, others, like myself, rotate their feet outward; causing a waddle, if you will. I have a look of horror on my face when he says the word *waddle*. I have never been accused of such a disgusting thing in my life. But before I can form a coherent response, he continues, "The extra . . . weight (and I'm sure that he pauses to emphasize the word) that the outside of the foot is forced to endure by walking incorrectly eventually causes it to grow an extra padding to help support the . . . load." Am I wrong or does he pause again when he says the word *load*?

Playing dumb, I ask, "And I'm getting one so young, why?"

Clearing his throat, Dr. Foster answers, "Well, a lot of it has to do with genetics and the structure of your foot." Then adds, "And a lot of it has to do with the extra weight (pause and meaningful look) you're placing on it."

I am so aghast by this whole conversation I finally confess, "I've just lost forty pounds." Which is a total lie by the way. In actuality I have just gained two. But I simply can't bear the humiliation of him calling me fat, or what I perceive as him calling me fat.

The doctor smiles and declares my previous poundage didn't help the inflammation at all and announces it may have contributed to my bunion. He checks his chart and declares, "I see you're a hundred-and-seventy pounds. At one fifty, you should be feeling a lot better."

"But I'm 5'11," I explain.

"Yes?"

"I'm big boned!"

He looks at me closely and says, "Actually, you're not." Picking up my wrist, he concludes, "I would say medium, which means one-hundred-and-fifty pounds would be ideal." Of course the photo of the emaciated woman on his desk should have tipped me off as to what this guy considers ideal. She's wearing a swimsuit with no boobs or butt to fill it out and painfully sharp collar bones. She bears a striking resemblance to an Auschwitz survivor.

All I can think is that I haven't been one-hundred-and fifty-pounds since high school. There is simply no way I can lose twenty pounds. I want to tell him he has no idea how much I deprive myself to weigh one seventy. In order to actually lose weight, I'd only be able to ingest rice cakes and Metamucil. But I don't say this because he'd think I'm weak and unmotivated and he'd be right, too. Plus, I just bragged that I lost a record forty pounds, so he already assumes I am capable of losing weight, which of course would be the truth if it weren't such an out-and-out lie.

The doctor writes a prescription for a special shoe insert that will help tip my foot into the correct walking position and then leaves, giving me privacy to cover my naked, misshapen appendage. As I put my sock back on I decide I am not going to go on a diet. I'm happy or happyish with the way I look and that's all there is to it. When I leave the room, Dr. Foster tells me to come back in two months so he can recheck my bunion. In my head I respond, "Yeah right, buddy. Take a good look, this is the last time you're ever going to see me or my growth." I plan on wearing my shoe insert and never again speaking of my hideous deformity.

The true cruelty of this whole bunion fiasco is that I am the one in my family with pretty feet. I have three sisters and we are all a year apart. Tell me that doesn't make for a crazy upbringing. At any rate, the year we were all in high school at the same time, my sisters and I were sitting on my bed having a nice familial chat, which was a rare occurrence as I'm sure you know girls that age are abominable as a whole. But put them under the same roof fighting over bathroom time, make-up, and let's not forget the all-important telephone. It was an ungodly ordeal to say the least.

My sisters, to my undying disgust, are all gorgeous and talented. Renée, the oldest one of the group is the unparalleled beauty of the family. Lest you think I'm exaggerating and she's not really all that *and* a bag of chips, let me ask if the name Renée Finnegan means anything to you? Yes, that's right, "The" Renée Finnegan, the gorgeous Midwestern girl that won the coveted Cover Girl contract when she was only seventeen, fresh out of high school. Try surviving two whole years at Pipsy High with people asking, "You're Renée's sister? Really?" The tone of incredulity was more than I could bear.

Next is Ginger. She's the brain. But please, before you picture an unfortunate looking nerd with braces and braids, I should tell you that she is only marginally less gorgeous than Renée. She was also the recipient of a Rhodes scholarship, which funded her degree in the history of Renaissance art, which she acquired at Oxford. Yes, Oxford, not the shoes, not the cloth, but the actual university in England.

The youngest of our quartet is Muffy, born Margaret Fay, but abbreviated to Muffy when at the tender age of two she couldn't pronounce Margaret Fay and began referring to herself as one might a forty-two-year old socialite. Muffy is the jock. She plays tennis and even enjoyed a run on the pro-circuit before a knee injury forced her to retire. She did, however, play Wimbledon three years in a row and, while she never actually won, the experience allows her to start sentences with, "Yes, well, when I played Wimbledon . . ." And make pronouncements like, "There's nothing like the courts at Wimbledon in the fall." Muffy is now the tennis pro at the Langley Country Club. Her husband Tom is the men's tennis pro, insuring they are the tannest, most fit couple on the entire planet. They're perfection is enough to make you barf.

I am the third child in my family, christened Miriam May Finnegan, which against my express consent got shortened to Mimi. For years I demanded, "It's Miriam, call me Miriam!" No one listened, as is the way in my family.

While sitting on my white quilted bedspread from JC Penny's, my sisters, in a moment of domestic harmony, decided we were all quite extraordinary. Renée was deemed the beautiful one, Ginger, the smart one, and Muffy, the athletic one. With those proclamations made, they appeared to be ready to switch topics when I demanded to know, "What am I?"

It's not that my sisters didn't love me. I don't think they thought I was troll-like or stupid, it's just compared to them, I didn't have any quality that outshone any one of theirs. So after much thoughtful consideration and examination, like a prized heifer at the state fair Renée announced, "You have the prettiest feet." Ginger and Muffy readily agreed.

Listen, I know you're thinking *prettiest feet* isn't something I should brag about. But in my family, I would have been thrilled to have the prettiest anything, and I am. They could have just as easily said I had the most blackheads, or the worst split ends. But they didn't, they awarded me prettiest feet and I was proud of it, until now. Now I have a bunion.

As I sit in front of my car in front of the Chesterton Medical Center, I become undone by the horror of having lost my identity in my family. "Who will I be now?" I wonder. Oh wait, I know, I'll be the spinster, or the one without naturally blonde hair, my true color hovering somewhere between bacon grease and baby poop. Hey wait, I know, I'll be the one who needs to lose twenty pounds!

The Reinvention of Mimi Finnegan, won a silver medal in the 2016 Readers' Favorite Awards, was a finalist in the RONE Awards, and won honorable mention at the London Book Festival.

Wilhelmina and the Willamette Wig Factory

Chapter One
Willy

Wilhelmina Snodgrass had red hair she hated, freckles she loathed, and with a name like Wilhelmina Snodgrass, why not just paint a target on her forehead and be done with it? Willy, as her friends called her, had just moved to Monteith with her mom, dad, and little brother, Wendell. Monteith was a historic town in the Willamette Valley in Oregon. She'd barely even heard of Oregon and now she lived here!

The first eleven-and-a-half years of her life were spent in a small farming town in central Illinois where the Snodgrass family was well-known and well-liked. So much so that no one in Mason even thought Snodgrass was a funny name anymore. Willy's dad worked for the John Deere tractor company. But darn her luck, he got a promotion that moved them all the way across the country. Did anyone ask Willy if she wanted to move? Nooooo. Did anyone think how hard it was going to be to make new friends in the summer time? Nooooo. It was like her vote didn't count for anything. So much for democracy, she fumed.

Willy was sitting on the stoop in front of her new house, sad, rejected, and madder than a wet hornet. The more she thought of it all, the madder she got. Wendell was already making new friends with a couple of boys down the street. But you know how boys are. They are not the least discriminating in their taste in friends. Boys will play with anything with two hands, two feet and a head. And in the case of Robbie Jakes back in Mason, one hand. To this day, Wendell wouldn't even think of playing with fireworks. Such is the effect that Robbie's misadventure had on him.

Willy sat on the stoop watching the movers unload the truck with a feeling of dread. Why did they have to move? Her life in Mason was perfect. She had two best friends, Bes and Ellie. She had a great bedroom *and* she was a shoo-in for the summer swim team. She had been practicing her backstroke for the past six months at the high school swimming pool and was better than any of the freshmen, and here she was just going into the seventh grade.

Was there a worse time to move than the seventh grade? If there was, Willy couldn't imagine it. In Mason, the seventh and eighth grades were in their own building and Willy couldn't wait to go to the junior high, directly across the street from the high school.

But here in the Willamette Valley, the sixth, seventh, and eighth grades shared a building. Being new, she was sure everyone would think she was a sixth-grader. Red hair, freckles, unfortunately named, and mistaken for a sixth-grader? Life couldn't possibly be any worse!

Emma Jean Snodgrass watched her daughter mope on the

front stoop. She felt really bad for her. A move was hard at any age, but eleven she thought, was a particularly difficult time in a girl's life. Not quite a child and not quite a teen, those tween years were a killer. She remembered all too well. Maybe she would take Willy to downtown Monteith and get her some new play clothes for the summer. That ought to cheer her up. When Emma Jean suggested the outing to Willy, she was greeted with, "Geez Mom, I'm almost twelve. We don't call them play clothes anymore."

"Okay dear, let me rephrase. Would you care to go shopping with your thoroughly ignorant, un-hip mom and buy some cool new summer threads?"

Willy rolled her eyes, "Sure, why not. It's not like I have any friends to hang out with."

So off they went, mother and daughter, on an expedition to make life better through shopping. The movers continued to move and John Snodgrass, Willy's dad, continued to direct the action. Wendell ran around the yard with his new friends screaming like a herd of banshees, and life in the Willamette Valley was now a reality.

On the drive through town, Willy realized two things. First off, Monteith wasn't that different from Mason. Both towns were pretty small, both had a bunch of churches, a park with a swimming pool, and the roads on both Main Streets were made of brick, from back in the horse and buggy days. Just as she was starting to feel a little at home, Willy thought about the second thing. As familiar as the town looked, she didn't know a soul in it.

It was like an episode of that old show her grandparents loved, *The Twilight Zone*. Everything was the same, but totally different. "Doo doo doo doo," she heard the show's theme song running through her head and she imagined a funny man in a dark suit walking out from behind a building saying, "You have now entered The Twilight Zone."

Willy's mom parked their mini-van on the street right in front of a store called The Glad Bag. The store looked pretty cool with a collection of low slung jeans in the window, belly shirts and lots of fun jewelry. Willy started to think the outing wasn't going to be so bad. When they walked in, a blast of cold air hit them and ever so slightly cooled her bad mood. A radically dressed teenager introduced herself as Charlene and told them that if they needed any direction with sizes and the like, she would be happy to help. Just when they started toward a rack of denim, Charlene looked Willy up and down and declared, "Hey Red, that is some of the coolest looking hair I've ever seen. Is that your real color or do you dye it?"

Shocked and pleased by the attention, Willy fibbed, "It's a rinse. I'm really a blonde."

Emma Jean looked at her daughter like she had grown a second head, but kept quiet and watched as her tween and this wild teenager continued their dialogue.

"No way! That is soooo cool! I love to do stuff with my hair. I just dyed my sister's hair blue with blueberry Jello and it's totally radical. Tommy's about your age. What are you, twelve?"

Willy answered, "I'll be twelve in August. I'm going into the seventh-grade in September."

Charlene brightened, "Then you have to know Tommy. She's going to be in the seventh-grade too."

"Well," Willy explained, "we just moved here from Illinois. I don't actually know anybody, yet."

Charlene started to refold some sweaters and said, "Listen Red, you gotta meet Tommy. She's one of the coolest kids in the junior high. She knows all the ins and outs and she'll give you the scoop on the Monteith social scene. Where do you live, anyway?"

Willy looked at her mom and answered, "We live on Carousel Lane, but I don't remember the house number."

Emma Jean cut in, "We live at number 231. It's the two story white Victorian with the wrap around porch."

Charlene interrupted with a, "NO WAY, we live at 238 Carousel! Well, that settles it. I'm gonna have Tommy come over this afternoon to introduce herself. You guys will hit it off like a train on fire!"

All of a sudden, Willy felt like there might be hope for her in Monteith, Oregon. She and her mom spent the next forty-five minutes shopping for summer clothes and in the end she took home a new hot pink bikini, two pairs of cropped pants, a halter top, and even a fake belly button ring. It was the belly button ring that made her realize her mom felt bad about the move. Had they still lived in Mason, she would have never approved that purchase.

Wilhelmina Rhonda Snodgrass started to think that there may, just may, be a light at the end of the tunnel. With any luck, that light might not be an oncoming train.

Wilhelmina and the Willamette Wig Factory was a finalist in the 2015 Readers' Favorite Awards.

49354442R00106

Made in the USA
San Bernardino, CA
22 May 2017